Edexcel GCSE

English and English Language

Extend

Student Book

Ron Norman
Danuta Reah
Racheal Smith
Consultant: **Geoff Barton**

A PEARSON COMPANY

Contents

Introduction

From Martin Phillips

Welcome to Edexcel English! We've worked hard to plan this course to make English engaging and exciting and to design assessments that really help you to show the skills you have developed.

Whether you're taking GCSE English or English Language you will have the opportunity to read and write texts about issues that are relevant to the world around you and to study both printed and on-screen texts, such as podcasts, trailers and websites. We expect you to have a personal opinion about all sorts of things you read and to be able to back up your opinion by giving good examples from the text. You have to write interestingly and engagingly in different genres and we also expect you to be able to both speak and listen in a variety of contexts.

This book has been designed to help you to get the best possible grade in GCSE English or English Language. It's tailored to helping students achieve the top grades and is full of tasks that will help you to get better at doing these various parts of English. We have tried to make these activities enjoyable and interesting and we hope they will encourage you to carry on reading, writing and communicating long after your GCSE English is done and dusted, as well as helping you to get a good grade in your GCSE.

Good luck with your studies and I hope you get the best possible results!

Martin Phillips

Martin Phillips, Senior Examiner for GCSE English

The Edexcel GCSE English and English Language specifications

Although GCSE English and GCSE English Language are separate qualifications, the Unit 1 controlled assessment task is common to both, and there are other common elements, including Speaking and Listening, and both have a practical writing task in the Unit 2 examination. Here is an overview of the specifications for both GCSE English and GCSE English Language:

Unit 1 English Today (English and English Language)

Controlled Assessment

What is this unit worth? 20% of the total marks

How long do students have? 4 hours (2 hours for each task)

What is the first task? Reading response to two on-screen or printed non-fiction texts on the same theme

What is the Reading task worth? 10% of the total marks

What is the second task? One non-fiction writing task on the same theme as the reading texts

What is the Writing task worth? 10% of the total marks

Unit 2 The Writer's Craft (English)

Exam

What is this unit worth? 40% of the total marks

How long is the exam? 2 hours

What is Section A? One three-part question based on an extract from a Shakespeare play you have studied

What is Section A worth? 10% of the total marks

What is Section B? One three-part question based on an extract from a Different Cultures novel you have studied

What is Section B worth? 10% of the total marks

What is Section C? One practical writing task

What is Section C worth? 20% of the total marks

Unit 2 The Writer's Voice (English Language)

Exam

What is this unit worth? 40% of the total marks

How long is the exam? 1 hour 45 minutes

What is Section A? One question on the language features of a non-fiction text or Different Cultures novel you have studied

What is Section A worth? 25% of the total marks

What is Section B? One practical writing task

What is Section B worth? 15% of the total marks

Unit 3 Creative English (English)

Controlled Assessment

What is this unit worth? 40% of the total marks

How long do students have? Up to 4 hours for the poetry reading task and the creative writing task (2 hours for each task)

What is the first task? Speaking and listening tasks: communicating and adapting language, interacting and responding, and creating and sustaining roles

What are the Speaking and Listening tasks worth? 20% of the total marks

What is the second task? A poetry reading task drawing on one literary heritage poem and at least two poems from the Anthology

What is the Poetry Reading task worth? 10% of the total marks

What is the third task? A creative writing task in response to a stimulus (e.g. an image, video clip or podcast)

What is the Creative Writing task worth? 10% of the total marks

Unit 3 Spoken Language (English Language)

Controlled Assessment

What is this unit worth? 40% of the total marks

How long do students have? Up to 4 hours for the spoken language study task and the writing for the spoken voice task (2 hours for each task)

What is the first task? Speaking and listening tasks: communicating and adapting language, interacting and responding, and creating and sustaining roles

What are the Speaking and Listening tasks worth? 20% of the total marks

What is the second task? A spoken language study based on two examples of spoken language

What is the Spoken Language Study worth? 10% of the total marks

What is the third task? One writing for the spoken voice task

What is the Writing for the Spoken Voice task worth? 10% of the total marks

Introduction

How is the book structured?

This book is divided into five units, each of which corresponds to one of the units in the English or English Language specification. Units 1 and 2 of this book are common to both GCSE English and GCSE English Language.

Specification	Unit	This book covers ...
English and English Language	Unit 1 English Today: Reading	the non-fiction Reading controlled assessment task.
	Unit 1 English Today: Writing	the non-fiction Writing controlled assessment task.
	Unit 2 The Writer's Craft / The Writer's Voice	the writing task in the exam (Section C of English and Section B of English Language).
English only	Unit 3 Creative English	the creative writing controlled assessment task.
English Language only	Unit 3 Spoken Language	the Spoken Language Study and the Writing for the Spoken Voice controlled assessment tasks.

Each unit is broken down into lessons, each of which opens with its own learning objectives. These introduce the skills, and are followed by stepped activities that help you develop the skills you need to achieve the top grades.

There are some activities that refer to additional digital resources, such as videos and podcasts, which are available on the ActiveTeach CD-ROM that accompanies this student book. These are to help you prepare for the options in the specifications for Unit 1 English Today and Unit 3 Creative English that require you to respond to or produce digital texts.

Assessment practice

At intervals throughout each unit there are Assessment practice activities that allow you to tackle an examination-style question or part of a controlled assessment task. These are followed by ResultsPlus Maximise your marks pages which provide sample student answers to the question you have attempted with examiner comments. You can read these before or after you grade your own response using the ResultsPlus: Self-assessment activity.

Regular ResultsPlus activities help students understand what they need to do to improve their grades.

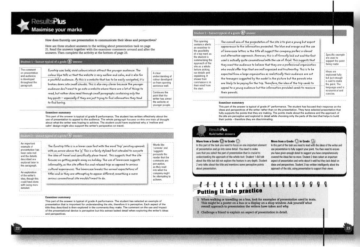

Putting it into practice activities suggest tasks you could complete to reinforce the skills you have learned.

At the end of each unit is a sample controlled assessment task or exam paper, so that you can see how you will be assessed. Mark schemes for these are available in the corresponding Teacher Guide. On the ActiveTeach CD-ROM there are interactive ResultsPlus grade improvement activities that include extracts from student responses at each band, with activities that help you to understand the differences between the bands and what you need to do to achieve better results.

ResultsPlus

These features combine expert advice and guidance from examiners to show you **how to achieve better results**. Many are based on insight gained from how students have performed in past assessments.

Build better answers – These give you an exam-style question or part of a controlled assessment task and help you to understand the mark scheme against which you will be assessed. They explain what you need to do in your response to the task to achieve the marks in each band. This book will show you what you need to do to achieve a mark in Band 3, 4 or 5 in your controlled assessment tasks and a mark in Band 1, 2 or 3 in the Higher Tier exam.

ResultsPlus
Build better answers

Look at this part of a controlled assessment task:
Explore how the writers communicate their ideas and perspectives.

■ A Band 3 answer will **clearly explore** the ideas and perspectives of the writer and will develop these to include **specific points with appropriate examples.**

● A Band 4 answer will include a **thorough exploration** of the ideas and perspectives of the writer. It is likely to give a selection of **detailed and appropriate examples to support the points made.**

▲ A Band 5 answer will include a **perceptive exploration** of the ideas and perspectives of the writer. It is likely to include **examples that fully support the points being made** and will be chosen with **discrimination.**

Self assessment – These help you to check your answers to activities to make sure that you have demonstrated the skills you will need to show in your assessment. The self assessment features that follow Assessment practice activities give you the opportunity to grade your answer using the mark scheme.

ResultsPlus
Self assessment

Check your answer – have you:

• picked out the main ideas from the text?
• summarised the overall point of the text?

Maximise your marks – These pages show examples of student work that is typical of what might be produced by students whose overall performance achieved one of the top grades. Some of these examples are taken from real student work from the Edexcel GCSE English pilot. These examples should help you to understand what you need to do to achieve your target grade.

Exam tip and Controlled assessment tip – These provide examiner advice and guidance to help improve your results.

ResultsPlus
Exam tip

▲ In your examination, use between 10% and 20% of the time available thinking, planning and checking. Use the remaining 80%-90% writing your answer.

Watch out! – These warn you about common mistakes and misconceptions that examiners frequently see students make. Make sure that you don't repeat them!

ResultsPlus
Watch out!

■ Be careful not to merely state what the writers have said in their texts. Remember to focus on the *use* of image, presentation and language and *how* this reveals the writer's perspective.

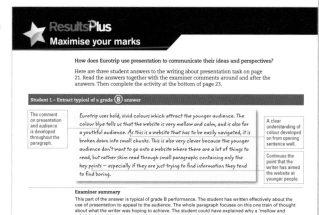

ResultsPlus
Maximise your marks

How does Eurotrip use presentation to communicate their ideas and perspectives?

Here are three student answers to the writing about presentation task on page 21. Read the answers together with the examiner comments around and after the answers. Then complete the activity at the bottom of page 23.

Student 1 – Extract typical of a grade Ⓑ answer

The comment on presentation and audience is developed throughout the paragraph.

Eurotrip uses bold, vivid colours which attract the younger audience. The colour blue tells us that the website is very mellow and calm, and is also for a youthful audience. As this is a website that has to be easily navigated, it is broken down into small chunks. This is also very clever because the younger audience don't want to go onto a website where there are a lot of things to read, but rather skim read through small paragraphs containing only the key points – especially if they are just trying to find information they tend to find boring.

A clear understanding of colour developed on from opening sentence well.

Continues the point that the writer has aimed the website at younger people.

Examiner summary
This part of the answer is typical of grade B performance. The student has written effectively about the use of presentation to appeal to the audience. The whole paragraph focuses on this one train of thought about what the writer was hoping to achieve. The student could have explained why a 'mellow and calm' design might also support the writer's perspective on travel.

Unit 1 English Today: Reading

Welcome to English Today, which is all about English in the world around you – the English you see and use every day of your life. In this student book, you will develop your skills in reading a range of non-fiction texts, some of them printed (such as posters, articles and reviews) and some of them on-screen (such as podcasts, trailers and websites).

This section of the book will help you to develop your reading skills, exploring how writers use presentation and language to communicate their ideas and perspectives to their readers. The texts and activities you will encounter in this book as you develop these skills are all focused on helping you to achieve your target grade in the reading part of your Unit 1 controlled assessment task.

Your assessment

Unit 1 is a controlled assessment unit. You will have two hours to complete one reading task. You can write up to 1000 words in your response to the task. The task will ask you to write about two different texts, on the same theme, from a choice of six. In order to prepare for your written response, you will have had the opportunity to study these texts in advance.

Your response to the task must show that you can:

✔ make comparisons between two texts

✔ select appropriate details from the texts to support your ideas

✔ explore how writers use presentation and language to communicate their ideas and perspectives.

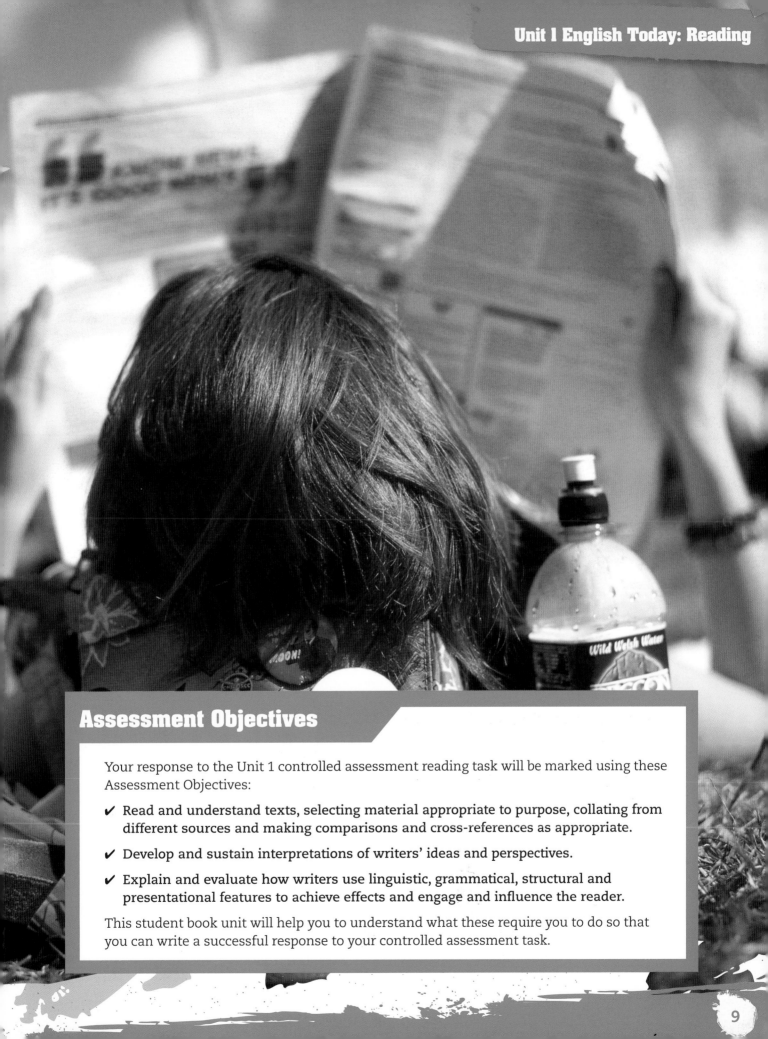

Assessment Objectives

Your response to the Unit 1 controlled assessment reading task will be marked using these Assessment Objectives:

✔ Read and understand texts, selecting material appropriate to purpose, collating from different sources and making comparisons and cross-references as appropriate.

✔ Develop and sustain interpretations of writers' ideas and perspectives.

✔ Explain and evaluate how writers use linguistic, grammatical, structural and presentational features to achieve effects and engage and influence the reader.

This student book unit will help you to understand what these require you to do so that you can write a successful response to your controlled assessment task.

1 Understanding main ideas

When you encounter any text in your Unit 1 Reading task or elsewhere, you should first aim to get an overall understanding of its main ideas. This is sometimes called reading for the **gist** of a text.

Activity 1

Read the article opposite and you'll see that its theme relates to the title of this unit: English Today.

1 Which of the statements below gives the most accurate summary of the ideas in the text?

 A The internet has transformed our lives in many ways and has allowed us to access a vast range of information quickly and efficiently.

 B Although the internet has been of tremendous benefit it has also changed the way we search and read information by reducing our powers of concentration.

 C The internet is slowly but surely interfering with people's brains and is reducing our intelligence.

 D The benefits of the internet outweigh the negative effects it has on our brains.

2 Which of the statements gives the least accurate summary of the ideas in the text?

3 Explain how you came to the decisions in Questions 1 and 2 and pick out relevant sections of the article to support your points.

In order to determine the gist of a text, it is also useful to identify the key points of the text. However, you will often encounter some parts of a text which are difficult to understand. When you do so, you can:

• make an educated guess from your broad understanding of the passage and the context in which they appear

• look up the words that are causing difficulty and express them using your own words.

Activity 2

Re-read the article on page 11.

1 Reduce its ideas to no more than five key bullet points.

2 Now use the context to make informed predictions about the meanings of the following two words from the text, choosing from the options suggested:

pithy	lengthy	funny	accurate	concise
foraging	browsing	hiding	looking for food	playing

Having identified your key points and the meaning of any unknown words, you can confirm your understanding of a text by trying to summarise it in your own words.

3 Try to do this for the article, writing roughly one paragraph.

Is Google Making Us Stupid?

Over the past few years I've had an uncomfortable sense that someone, or something, has been tinkering with my brain, remapping the neural circuitry, reprogramming the memory. My mind isn't going – so far as I can tell – but it's changing. I'm not thinking the way I used to think. I can feel it most strongly when I'm reading. Immersing myself in a book or a lengthy article used to be easy. My mind would get caught up in the narrative or the turns of the argument, and I'd spend hours strolling through long stretches of prose. That's rarely the case anymore. Now my concentration often starts to drift after two or three pages. I get fidgety, lose the thread, begin looking for something else to do. I feel as if I'm always dragging my wayward brain back to the text. The deep reading that used to come naturally has become a struggle.

I think I know what's going on. For more than a decade now, I've been spending a lot of time online, searching and surfing and sometimes adding to the great databases of the Internet. The Web has been a godsend to me as a writer. Research that once required days in the stacks or periodical rooms of libraries can now be done in minutes. A few Google searches, some quick clicks on hyperlinks, and I've got the telltale fact or pithy quote I was after. Even when I'm not working, I'm as likely as not to be foraging in the Web's 'info-thickets' reading and writing e-mails, scanning headlines and blog posts, watching videos and listening to podcasts, or just tripping from link to link to link. …

For me, as for others, the Net is becoming a universal medium, the conduit for most of the information that flows through my eyes and ears and into my mind. … And what the Net seems to be doing is chipping away my capacity for concentration and contemplation. My mind now expects to take in information the way the Net distributes it: in a swiftly moving stream of particles. Once I was a scuba diver in the sea of words. Now I zip along the surface like a guy on a Jet Ski.

An active reader will always reflect on what is implied by the ideas in a text, and question them. In this article, the writer has proposed some provocative ideas about the impact of the internet on the way we think.

Activity 3

The writer neatly summarises the ideas expressed in the article by using both a metaphor and a simile in the final two sentences.

> Once I was a scuba diver in the sea of words. Now I zip along the surface like a guy on a Jet Ski.

1 **What do you think the writer implies by using these images?**

2 **How convincing do you find the writer's argument about the impact of the internet on the way people think? Write a paragraph explaining how convincing you think his argument is.**

2 Understanding perspective

An important part of understanding the texts in your controlled assessment is recognising the attitude and point of view (or **bias**) of the writer. This means asking questions such as:

- Does the writer express positive or negative attitudes and opinions on the topic in the text?
- Does the writer offer a balanced view in the text, or is it one-sided or biased?
- What is the viewpoint that the writer wishes his or her readers to share?

Sometimes it is easy to see the writer's perspective, but often it is implied by the use of language and presentation rather than stated openly.

ResultsPlus
Build better answers

Look at this controlled assessment task:
Explore how the writers communicate their ideas and perspectives.

■ A Band 3 answer will **clearly explore** the ideas and perspectives of the writer and will develop these to include **specific points with appropriate examples**.

● A Band 4 answer will include a **thorough exploration** of the ideas and perspectives of the writer. It is likely to give a selection of **detailed and appropriate examples to support the points made**.

▲ A Band 5 answer will include a **perceptive exploration** of the ideas and perspectives of the writer. It is likely to include **examples that fully support the points being made** and will be chosen with **discrimination**.

Activity 1

1 Look at the Crimestoppers poster and state what is implied about:

a) the writer's attitude towards knife crime

b) what the writer thinks young people can do to protect themselves

c) how much the police depend on informants

d) young people's feelings about 'informing' the police

e) what the writer thinks about the act of informing the police.

In your controlled assessment, you will be asked to compare the perspectives expressed in two contrasting texts.

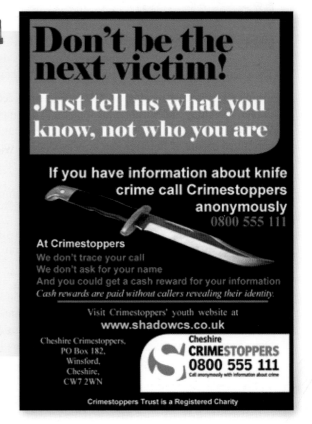

Activity 2

Read Texts A and B opposite about animal welfare.

1 Explain what seems to be the perspective of each text on the issue of animal welfare.

2 Explain how the following key aspects of each text help to convey the writer's perspective:

a) the use of images

b) the way the text is presented (layout and font)

c) the use of language.

Some people use her as a milk machine. They see her as a piece of property, and keep her in a tiny stall. She's a mother, but they'll take away all her children. They'll kill her when she is six, though she'd naturally live to be 20.

PLEASE HELP HER.

Text A

Text B

Meet the dairy farmer who pampers his 'happy' cows with waterbeds and flat-screen TVs

When it comes to comfort, the cows of U.S. farmer Kirk Christie have it all – a new barn, a flat-screen television and waterbeds.

That's because of the dairy farmer's philosophy that a happy cow is a productive cow. More milk means more money, so Christie doesn't mind providing the frills.

"Them cows are my girls," said Christie, who runs a farm near Slater, about 25 miles (40 kilometers) north of Des Moines. "You ask anybody, I probably think more highly of those cows than I do myself."

Christie's 23 cows spend about 18 hours a day on waterbeds he installed in November.

He said the beds, durable rubber mats that lie flat on the ground and are filled with water, were popular with the animals from the beginning.

They provide heat for the cows in the winter and coolness in the summer, depending on the water Christie pipes in.

Activity 3

1 Explain in two to three paragraphs how convincing you find each text and which one (if any) you find yourself most closely in sympathy with.

Look at these comments from other students as a starting point.

Text A	Text B
The image makes us look her right in the eye… It makes me feel guilty.	He's not really bothered about the cows. It's all about getting more milk!

3 Identifying audience and purpose

This lesson will help you to...

→ understand how a text reflects its audience and purpose

The choices a writer makes are driven by two key factors:

- who the text is aimed at (its **audience**)
- what the text is aiming to do to the audience (its **purpose**).

To understand how language is being used in any of the texts in your controlled assessment, you always need to bear the audience and purpose in mind.

When thinking about the **audience** of a text, there are two key questions to consider:

1 Who does this text seem to be aimed at? The answer could be a group of people defined according to:

- their age group
- their gender
- their background.

2 What does the text assume about its readers – their interests, their knowledge and their attitudes?

Activity

Look at this horoscope from Mizz magazine.

ResultsPlus

Controlled assessment tip

Try to think about the possible interests and backgrounds of the audience of a text, as well as their age and gender.

YOUR YEAR AHEAD

LEO

The good news is that the year to come is all about love, lads and flirting for you, Leo! You know how to have fun with all of that, so your immediate future should be full of giggles and crushes – just as you like it! Friendships and your social life will be one big party, too.

HIGHLIGHTS Love, crushes, fab mates, parties and fun. School should go well if you work hard.

LOWLIGHTS Be cautious or you could have money troubles. Family relationships are strained at times.

1 Identify the intended audience of this text.

2 What does the text seem to assume about the interests, values and lifestyle of this audience?

Having noted the intended audience of a text, the next thing you should consider is its **purpose**. The answer could be one, or more, of the following:

- convey information or instructions which the audience needs
- educate the audience
- influence the audience in some way – by arguing for an idea, persuading them to do something, or advising them
- entertain the audience – by amusing, moving or intriguing them.

Part of your task in the controlled assessment will be to consider how the purpose(s) of a text have influenced the language choices made by the writer.

Activity ② Read Texts A and B.

Text A

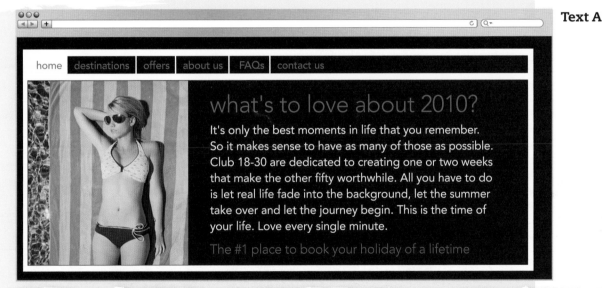

home | destinations | offers | about us | FAQs | contact us

what's to love about 2010?

It's only the best moments in life that you remember. So it makes sense to have as many of those as possible. Club 18-30 are dedicated to creating one or two weeks that make the other fifty worthwhile. All you have to do is let real life fade into the background, let the summer take over and let the journey begin. This is the time of your life. Love every single minute.

The #1 place to book your holiday of a lifetime

Back from the dead *I ain't afraid of no ghosts*

Text B

Ghostbusters: the video game

They're back! This game, set in 1991 and written by Dan Aykroyd and Harold Ramis, heralds the return of the Ghostbusters. All the familiar characters feature, but you play the 'new guy' exploring the surreal and spooky surroundings of New York. You hunt down ghosts, destroy hotel lobbies, and try not to cross streams while your buddies wisecrack. Unfortunately, the slightly dated lip-synching make your mates look like plastic mannequins. For the most part, though it's sharp and well presented, and while it's a pretty standard action-adventure, it's great fun to play for anyone who remembers the glory days of this group of ghost terminators.

1 Identify the possible audience(s) for each text.

2 Explain what each text assumes about its readers.

3 Explain in two paragraphs what the purpose of each text is. Remember that each text might have more than one purpose. Pick out examples of language, images, or presentation which help you to understand the purposes of the texts.

4 Understanding presentation and its effects

This lesson will help you to...

→ understand presentational devices used by writers and speakers

→ analyse the effect of these devices

In your controlled assessment task you need to comment in some detail on how a text presents ideas and information to its readers. You might explore the way a text is organised on the page (**layout**), the use of different **presentational devices**, such as varied print sizes, fonts and other graphic devices, and the use of **colour**. You will also need to consider the use of **images**, which are explored in more depth on pages 24–25.

However, it is important that you do more than simply describe the presentation of a text – you also need to explain what these features imply and how the design choices made by the producers of the text contribute to its meanings, fulfil the text's purpose and connect with its audience.

Activity ①

Study the pages below taken from a magazine called *JobFresh*, designed to help jobseekers find employment.

1 Write two to three paragraphs in response to the following question:

> **How do the presentational devices help the text achieve its purpose and reach its audience?**

Break down your answer to this question by following the annotations below.

Typography
How do the different fonts and text sizes contribute to the accessibility of the text?

Colour
Why do you think the magazine uses a set combination of bright colours?

Layout
How does the use of subheadings, text boxes, bullets, extra spacing or text wraparound make the text accessible and attractive for the audience?

Images
Why have these images been included? How are they presented and how does their size effect the impact they make?

Best job by degrees

The graduate marketplace is a highly competitive place. So, what can you do to increase your chances of getting a great job?

Leaving behind the world of alcohol, late nights and licentiousness for a proper job can be a shock to the system – but the rewards and responsibility can be very fulfilling.

Most graduates look for the same criteria when selecting a job. Salary is, of course, key but so too is the opportunity there will be for ongoing training and development, how much real responsibility is on offer, work/life balance, your holiday allocation, and a host of key extras from health insurance to pension schemes.

Graduate development programmes
Many leading Blue Chips and corporations are driven to get hold of the cream of the graduate crop and will do a lot to secure their ideal candidates. They may offer salaries that many work for years to achieve and run graduate development programmes over 2 to 5 years to carry loyalty and engender belonging.

Get a foot in the door
However, for many smaller businesses belt-tightening is a must and employees lower down the career hierarchy are being asked to take on

Job: Cartographer
Duration: 20 years
I enjoy the challenge of producing maps that people can use for a specific purpose: people love maps.

more responsibility – squeezing the amount of graduate jobs available. Today, there are more graduates and less suitable posts so adjusting expectations and getting a foot in the door may be your best chance.

Be patient
Horizontal promotion is far more prevalent today when you do secure a career so be patient as you may not be able to pay off that student loan over night. What could mark you out for promotion is if you continue to learn on the job and gain new skills through training. Remember, your career path is down to you alone and the more initiative you show the more likely you are to get ahead.

FACT: The man who invented police fingerprinting was from Staffordshire? His name was Dr Henry Faulds.

The top 9 reasons to be happy at work

- Friendly colleagues
- Rewarding work
- Good boss
- Great work/life balance
- Diversity of role
- Doing something with intrinsic value like charity work
- Making a difference
- Part of a successful set-up or team
- Competitive salary

Source: Chiumento's Happiness at Work Index

There are dozens of possible fonts available. Every font has its own impact, implications and **connotations**. The fonts chosen for a particular text will reflect:

- the degree of seriousness or formality the writer wishes to convey
- how modern the writer wants the text to feel
- the writer's relationship with their audience.

Activity 2

Consider the four example texts in the table on the right, which have been created using distinctive fonts.

1 For each piece of text, explain why the use of the font could be seen as inappropriate.

With deepest sympathy on the loss of your loved one	PCs repaired and upgraded Software installed Broadband connections
Official Notice: Trespassers will be prosecuted	Ye Olde Antique Shoppe Bric-a-brac and antiques

In the case of **spoken texts** such as podcasts, it is still possible to discuss presentation. You can comment on use of sound or voice designed to enhance the listening experience. These will include a number of **aural** and **vocal** devices:

Written texts	Spoken text equivalent
Headings, headlines and subheadings	Use of announcements at the 'top' of the piece and throughout and introductions of speakers/interviewees e.g. *'Coming up in the next hour we have…'*
Use of varied fonts and type-size	Use of different speakers and tones of voices *How do the voices in the podcast interact and vary the pace of the audio in order to create the appropriate style? Are there variations in the pitch and tone of voice?*
Use of colour, images and other graphic devices	Use of sound effects (SFX) and/or music in the background *How does the choice of music contribute to the tone of the piece?*

In this month's podcast we find out how quitting smoking could leave you happier as well as healthier…

CANCER RESEARCH UK

Activity 3

Listen to a podcast such as the Cancer Research UK podcast about the cancer risks related to smoking and tanning available on the ActiveTeach.

1 Make notes about how the podcast makes use of the different devices outlined in the table above. Pick out specific examples.

5 Commenting on presentation

This lesson will help you to...

→ write about presentation

→ make meaningful and analytical comments that do not just describe a text

It is relatively easy to describe how presentational devices contribute to the meanings of a text, but to achieve the higher grades in your controlled assessment you need to write perceptively about these with brief, supporting examples. This means that it's not enough simply to say which devices a text uses; you need to explain how, and why, these devices have been chosen. It is also important to use clear, precise language in your answer, including any technical terminology that helps you to define your points exactly.

Activity 1

Look at the technical terms given below along with their definitions.

1 Find a text (this could be a newspaper or magazine article, an online text, a poster or a leaflet) in which at least two of these features are used.

2 Write two to three paragraphs explaining the effect of these features within your text, focusing on how they are appropriate for its audience and purpose(s).

Signposting
Any devices used to guide audience around a written text or audio.

Typography
Variations in the size, type and range of fonts used.

Foregrounding
Making a feature the most prominent on the page by bringing it to the 'front'.

Anchoring
Use of text to interpret an image and give it meaning for the audience.

In addition to the presentational devices found in print-based texts, **webpages** use a number of special features:

- corporate logo/design features
- index of links to other pages within the site
- static and moving images
- hyperlinks to other sites
- navigation bars.

Activity 2

To practise writing about presentation, look at the webpage below which appears on Cancer Research UK's Bobby Moore Fund website.

1 Work out the main ideas the webpage is conveying, its purpose(s) and its target audience.

2 Make notes in preparation for a longer piece of writing about how and why presentational devices are used to communicate the ideas and perspectives of the text.

Once you have picked out some interesting features to comment on from the text you are studying, you need to write your ideas down clearly and accurately. For each significant point you make, it might be helpful to create a separate well-structured paragraph, as shown in the following table.

ResultsPlus
Controlled assessment tip

Instead of saying that some presentational devices make the text stand out, say that the device emphasises that part of the text. Then, you must explain why that part of the text should be emphasised to the reader.

Paragraph structure	Example
1 Make your basic point clearly in a single well-constructed sentence. This is the **topic sentence** for the paragraph.	The writers of this text have used a consistent colour scheme which links with the colours of the charity's logo.
2 Go on to refer specifically to a **detail** from the text and use the relevant **terminology**.	For example, the menu bar, the title and subtitle, the logo on the left and the two images on the page all use the same shade of red.
3 The vital bit – now go on to **explain** how, or why, or with what effect…	This helps to create coherence and an impression of modernity and professionalism which helps to instil confidence in the charity and the work that they do.

ResultsPlus
Self assessment

Check your answer – have you:

- been discriminating in the examples of presentation that you will explore?

- commented on the impact of the presentation, linking to the writer's intention?

- commented in detail on each example you have selected?

Activity ❸

1 Turn the notes you made for Activity 2 into a number of well developed paragraphs using the method shown in the table above.

As part of your controlled assessment task you could explore how the writers communicate their ideas and perspectives using presentation.

Activity 4

First identify both the audience and purpose of the website to the right. Then write a response to this question:

How does Eurotrip use presentation to communicate its ideas and perspectives?

You should spend 10 minutes on this task.

ResultsPlus
Self assessment

Before you complete this self-assessment activity, you might like to read some sample answers to this task on the following pages (22 – 23).

1 Check your answer to Activity 4:

- Did you use the most appropriate examples of presentation?
- Did you name and comment in detail on the specific item of presentation you selected?
- Did you link the writer's use of presentation to their ideas and perspective, considering the intended impact on the reader?

2 Now decide which Band your answer to Activity 4 falls into by applying the mark scheme opposite. You will need to be careful and precise in your marking.

Band 3

- selects appropriate examples of presentational devices to comment on and the examples chosen show some support of the points being made
- comments on presentation are sound
- includes clear exploration of the ideas and perspectives of the writer

Band 4

- selects appropriate small parts of the presentational devices to focus on in detail and the examples chosen support the points being made
- comments on presentation are detailed
- thoroughly explores the ideas and perspectives of the writer

Band 5

- selects well-chosen examples that fully support the point being made
- comments on presentation are perceptive
- perceptive exploration of the ideas and perspectives of the writer

Maximise your marks

How does Eurotrip use presentation to communicate its ideas and perspectives?

Here are three student answers to the writing about presentation task on page 21. Read the answers together with the examiner comments around and after the answers. Then complete the activity at the bottom of page 23.

Student 1 – Extract typical of a grade B answer

The opening comment on presentation and audience is then developed throughout the paragraph.

> Eurotrip uses bold, vivid colours which attract the younger audience. The colour blue tells us that the website is very mellow and calm, and is also for a youthful audience. As this is a website that has to be easily navigated, it is broken down into small chunks. This is also very clever because the younger audience don't want to go onto a website where there are a lot of things to read, but rather skim read through small paragraphs containing only the key points – especially if they are just trying to find information they tend to find boring.

An understanding of colour developed on well from opening sentence.

Continues the point that the writer has aimed the website at younger people.

Examiner summary

This part of the answer is typical of a grade B performance. The student has written effectively about the use of presentation to appeal to the audience. The whole paragraph focuses on this one train of thought about what the writer was hoping to achieve. The student could have explained why a 'mellow and calm' design might also support the writer's perspective on travel.

Student 2 – Extract typical of a grade A answer

An important example of presentation has been selected and the details described are explored later in the paragraph.

> The Eurotrip title is in a lowercase font with the word 'trip' pointing upwards with an arrow above the 'p.' This is a fairly stylised font intended to connote the idea of travel and specifically air travel. This suggests that the site focuses on getting people away on holiday. The use of lower case suggests informality, as the site offers fun and relaxed trips as opposed to serious cultural experiences. The lower case breaks the normal expectations of titles and so they are attempting to appear different, something a more serious conventional site wouldn't want to do.

Words like 'connote' and 'suggests' help to show that the student has read into what the company might be attempting to achieve.

An exploration of the writer's perspective, though the student could have explored this in more detail.

Examiner summary

This part of the answer is typical of a grade A performance. The student has selected an example of presentation that is important for understanding the site. Each aspect of the title they described is then explored in the comments they make. The student makes good comments on the use and impact of the presentational device but this extract lacked detail when exploring the writer's ideas and perspectives.

This opening sentence alerts an examiner to the possibility of a top mark as the student is summarising the overall approach of the site before picking out details and explaining. It shows their conclusion is in their mind from the start.

The overall aim of the presentation of the site is to give a young but expert appearance to the information presented. The blue and orange and the use of lowercase letters in the title all suggest the company prefers a vibrant and alternative approach. However, this is all formally laid out and the font used is actually quite conventional with the use of Arial. This suggests that they want the audience to believe that they are a professional organisation who would offer trips that are well organised and trustworthy. This is to be expected from a large organisation as realistically their audience are not the teenagers suggested by the model in the picture but the parents who are likely to be paying for the trip. Therefore, the idea of the trip needs to appeal to a young audience but the information provided needs to reassure their parents.

Specific example is used to support the point being made.

Ideas are explained fully but just enough is said to make the point. The language used is economical and concise.

Examiner summary

This part of the answer is typical of a grade A* performance. The student has focused their response on the ideas and perspectives of the writer rather than on the presentation. They have selected presentation that fully supports the points that they are making. The points made about the audience and the approach of the site are explored carefully while choosing only the parts of the text that help to build their points.

ResultsPlus
Build better answers

Move from a Grade Ⓑ to Grade Ⓐ

In this part of the task you need to focus on one important element of presentation and go into some detail. You need to make sure that you select the part of presentation that is crucial to understanding the approach of the whole text. Student 1 did talk about the title but did not explore the feature in any depth. Student 2 only talks about the title and mentions some observant points about presentation.

Aim for a Grade Ⓐ*

In this part of the task you need to lead with the ideas of the writer and use presentation to fully support your point. You then need to ensure you have given enough detail to suggest you have comprehensively covered the ideas but no more. Student 2 does select an important aspect of presentation and writes about it well but they lack detail on ideas and perspectives. Student 3 has written intelligently about the approach of the site, using presentation to support their views.

Putting it into practice

1   When walking, or travelling on a bus, look for examples of presentation used in advertisements. Ask yourself what overall approach to presentation the writers have taken and why.

2   Explain an aspect of presentation in detail to a friend.

6 Understanding how images are used

Some of the texts you will encounter in the controlled assessment are likely to include images, and you need to be able to discuss their use in your response to the task. There are usually three questions to consider:

1 **What ideas or information does the image convey or imply?** This could mean looking at aspects of the image itself such as:
   - subject matter
   - composition
   - use of colour
   - camera angle and point of view.

2 **Why is the image being used?** This could be to:
   - convey an aspect of the text more vividly
   - attract the reader's attention so they will go on to read the text
   - influence the way readers respond to the text.

3 **What is the relationship between image and text?** This could involve asking:
   - how essential to the text is the image?
   - does the text refer to the image directly or indirectly?
   - does the text or caption interpret the image for the reader?

ResultsPlus
Controlled assessment tip

Writing about colour and image offers the opportunity for more perceptive comments than those simply focusing on devices such as bold font, italics or bullet points.

Activity 1

Look at the Innocent drinks poster opposite and answer these questions.

1 What ideas does the image convey or imply?
   a) How does the composition of the image ensure the fruit dominates?
   b) Comment on the **camera angle** used and the point of view it offers the reader.
   c) How does the choice of **colours** (in both the fruit and the background) contribute to the impact of the advert?

2 Why is the image being used?
   a) What impact is the advert designed to achieve?
   b) Is it more, or less, effective than showing just an image of a smoothie?

3 What is the relationship between the image and the text?
   a) How does the text affect the way you interpret the image?
   b) What is unusual about the language used?

Activity ❷

Consider the poster to the right, designed as part of a public awareness campaign addressing burns and scalds among babies and young children. You should now be able to write your own response to the question:

> **How have the producers of this text used the image to help communicate their ideas and perspectives?**

1 Start by breaking down the question as you did with the Innocent advert above.

2 Now write two paragraphs commenting on how the image is used in this public awareness poster.

ResultsPlus
Watch out!

When writing about images, be careful not to just describe what you see. Remember to comment on *why* the image has been selected using words such as *because*, *suggests* or *implies*.

7 Understanding moving images

This lesson will help you to...

→ understand, describe and analyse the effects of moving images

You might be asked to explore a moving image in your controlled assessment task. Moving images might be advertisements, trailers or animations. 'Reading' moving images involves understanding some of the choices the director has made and thinking about their effectiveness in terms of their intended audience and purpose.

These choices include:

- **Editing:** Does the piece cut rapidly between different images/scenes/camera positions, or stay with just one or two?
- **Composition:** What is placed in the foreground? Where is the viewer meant to look? Is the camera still, or does it follow (or track) the action? Is it in close up or long shot? Does it zoom in or out?
- **Colour and lighting:** Is it bright or shadowy? What colours are used?
- **Sound and music:** What kinds of sound and music are used?
- **Speech:** Is any dialogue used? What use is made of voiceover?

Activity 1

Watch a trailer for a film or a short TV advert such as the 'Be Humankind' advert for Oxfam available on the ActiveTeach.

1 Explain what you think are the purpose(s) and audience of the piece.

2 Now consider the choices made by the directors of the piece, and their effects, as shown in the notes below.

Speech and text
Select sections of text are used in visually innovative ways in much of the advert, meaning that speech is not necessary. Only three linked phrases are spoken at the end of the advert. How does the choice of text and speech and how they are presented affect the audience and help achieve the advert's purpose?

Editing
At first there is swift cutting between shots and a variety of camera angles are used but later on the camera pauses for an extended amount of time on a key image. Why have these decisions been made and how do they help to communicate the message of the advert?

Composition
At first the shots are all close ups, and the camera tracks the action. Later wide-angle shots predominate. Why is this? How does it fit with the purpose of the advert?

Colour and lighting
Predominantly greens, browns and blues are used at the start, but at a point towards the end bright white light appears followed by explosive colour. How does this use of colour help to convey meaning?

Sound and music
Quiet rhythmic music at the start gives way to a monotone sound, followed by a more lively, louder and faster piece at the end. Why have these decisions been made?

As part of your controlled assessment task you could explore how the writers use images as presentational devices to communicate their ideas and perspectives.

Activity 2

First identify both the audience and purpose of the website to the right. Then write a response to this question:

How does Eurotrip use images to communicate its ideas and perspectives?

You should spend 10 minutes on this task.

ResultsPlus
Self assessment

Before you complete this self-assessment activity you might like to read some sample answers to this task on the following pages (28 – 29).

1 Check your answer to Activity 2:

- Did you select small parts of images to comment on?
- Did you only describe those parts of the image that are relevant to the point you are making?
- Did you link the writer's use of image to their ideas and perspective, considering the intended impact on the reader?

2 Now decide which Band your answer to Activity 2 falls into by applying the mark scheme opposite. You will need to be careful and precise in your marking.

■ **Band 3**

- selects images to comment on and clearly links the examples to the points being made
- comments on images are sound and show the point being developed
- makes clear links between the images used and the writer's ideas and perspectives

● **Band 4**

- selects small parts of the images to focus on in detail
- comments on images are detailed
- makes thorough comments on the links between the images used and the writer's ideas and perspectives of the ideas within the text

▲ **Band 5**

- selects well-chosen examples that fully support the point being made
- comments on image are perceptive
- perceptive exploration of the ideas and perspectives of the writer

Maximise your marks

How does Eurotrip use images to communicate its ideas and perspectives?

Here are three student answers to the writing about image task on page 27. Read the answers together with the examiner comments around and after the answers. Then complete the activity at the bottom of page 29.

Direct connection between perspective in the website and the image, which is then explored more thoroughly with the use of 'therefore' to add further detail.

> Eurotrip has a picture of a teenager surrounded by European landmarks. This suggests that the website can guide teenagers on their journey around Europe. The different landmarks suggest he can go to any one of these places therefore does not limit his destination to one city. The boy is looking carefully at a map to work out where to go next but he seems confident – this might be because the website has given him confidence to travel and select destinations when he is there.

A comment which links the image to the purpose of the text.

Examiner summary

This part of the answer is typical of a grade B performance. This student has used words such as 'therefore' which show that they are adding detail to the ideas they are writing. The final sentence could have been written more confidently, removing the word 'might', but it does add further detail to the comment about the picture so it explores the main purpose of the website – which is to make travellers feel safe and confident when travelling.

This is a good observation which is analysed well.

> The designer has cleverly used spots of orange and blue on the map in the model's hand. This links to the blue and orange of the website and means that the reader links the confidence of the man with Eurotrip. The reader would want to be like the man because he looks attractive. However, the look on his face is a little perplexed. This could be from the overwhelming choice of places he has to go thanks to the website. Yet it could also suggest that he is lost – not the best advertisement for a travel website. It is likely that the designers wanted to encourage an idea of adventure and the look on the attractive model's face may be seen as someone overwhelmed by choice.

This point is developed but needs to be expressed in a more concise way.

Examiner summary

This part of the answer is typical of a grade A performance. The comment about the orange and blue spots on the map is observant. These details show potential A* quality. However, the comment about the model, though well developed, does not show the discrimination of the top grade. Therefore, the student needed to think this point through further to elevate their answer from that typical of an A grade to that typical of an A*.

> The comment picks up on the main ideas and perspectives of the website.

> The points support the main idea of the paragraph well.

The website uses images to evoke the idea of travel and adventure. The most obvious images to suggest travel are the iconic landmarks that represent different European cities. More powerful is the image of the mountain and blue sky which is symbolic of adventure and freedom. The large amount of blue sky in the image suggests that there is a lot of space to explore. The designer has purposefully created a theme that will excite the reader into wanting to go on a trip of some kind. Eurotrip's ability to organise this trip is suggested by the splash of blue and orange, the corporate colours of the site, on the map held by the model. He is clearly being guided around Europe with the help of the company.

Examiner summary

This part of the answer is typical of a grade A* performance. The student has explored the idea that the website is promoting excitement in the reader at the idea of travel and adventure. They develop their response, first when discussing the image of the mountain and then with the use of blue and orange. The student makes careful reference to relevant images.

 ResultsPlus
Build better answers

**Move from a Grade to Grade **

In this part of the task you need to make sure you consider the primary purpose of the text and how the image is used to suggest this. Student 1 makes good comments about the website but the main point of the paragraph is the impact of the image and not the idea it represents. Student 2 begins with a point that focuses on the aim of the website to promote the services of Eurotrip.

**Aim for a Grade **

In this part of the task you need to make sure you sustain the quality of the ideas throughout the response. Student 2 made a point with an example that fully supported their idea. However, the student then attempted to expand on this idea and needed to be more concise to demonstrate the discrimination of the top grade.

Putting it into practice

1   Explain to a partner how to achieve an A grade.

2   Design a poster which aims to persuade families to travel to a particular destination with your travel company. Think about the kind of language, presentation and images you will use.

3   Explain to a friend exactly why you have designed your poster in the way you have.

8 Understanding language choices: vocabulary

This lesson will help you to...

→ understand and describe the choices of vocabulary made in texts

→ analyse the effects of these choices

In your controlled assessment task you will need to comment closely on how words are used to convey ideas and perspectives to the reader.

The **vocabulary** a writer chooses will reveal a great deal about the ideas and perspective of a text. It may include a variety of vocabulary choices:

- words that are clearly biased or designed to create a positive or negative emotional reaction (**emotive** language)

- **similes**, **metaphors** or other imagery or comparisons that convey the writer's ideas or feelings

- the deliberate use of exaggeration to make a point (**hyperbole**)

- the use of **irony** or sarcasm

- the use of **quotations**

- **formal** or **informal** vocabulary, such as scientific/specialist language (formal) or slang words (informal).

Look at the extract from Stuart Maconie's book *Pies and Prejudice* below, in which he conveys his personal impressions of London and compares these with earlier views expressed by well-known poets.

Wordsworth famously said of the view from Westminster Bridge that 'earth has not anything to show more fair.' This is mental, particularly from someone who lived in the Lake District, where there is something more fair around every hummock. I mean, it's all right. There's a big greasy-looking river and some tugs and the odd dredger. There's the London Eye, a piece of London that is forever Blackpool, and there's the rather handsome old GLC building. On the other side there's a couple of flash office blocks and Big Ben, of course. So, all in all, you know, pretty good but 'earth has not anything to show more fair'? Mental. His mate Thomas de Quincey put it rather differently: 'A duller spectacle this earth of ours has not to show than a rainy Sunday in London.' Another lake poet chum, Percy Bysshe Shelley, was even harsher: 'Hell is a city much like London.'

I wouldn't go that far but I, like most northerners, maintain a cordial suspicion of 'the Smoke', even though I must have spent months there since my first visit.

Activity ❶

1 Identify both the audience and purpose(s) of the text.

2 Summarise in your own words Maconie's overall ideas and perspectives on the city of London.

3 Now write sentences about how the following words and phrases from the text convey Maconie's perspective and reflect his target audience and purpose(s). The first has been completed as an example.

a) 'This is mental'

> The colloquial term 'mental', used twice in the extract, forcefully suggests that he does not share the poet Wordsworth's high opinion of the city. It contrasts strongly with the formal traditional language used in Wordsworth's quotations and therefore creates an amusing tone, which helps him achieve his purpose of entertaining his audience.

b) 'I mean, it's all right'

c) 'There's a big greasy-looking river and some tugs and the odd dredger'

d) 'There's the London Eye, a piece of London that is forever Blackpool'

4 Identify two more words or phrases that convey the writer's perspective and reflect the audience and purpose(s) of the text. Explain how they do this.

ResultsPlus
Controlled assessment tip

When preparing for your controlled assessment, practise adapting language terms so that they fit grammatically into sentences. For instance, make sure that you're clear on when you would use 'ironic' as opposed to 'irony', 'personified' rather than 'personification' and 'colloquialism' rather than 'colloquial'. For example, you can say that the word 'mental' is a colloquial term (this is use of the *adjective*), but you would say that the term 'mental' is a colloquialism (this is use of the *noun*).

Activity ❷

In the text, Stuart Maconie refers to three earlier writers who had different views of the capital – William Wordsworth, Thomas de Quincey and Percy Bysshe Shelley. You may need to do some research to find out who they were and when they wrote their comments.

1 What does the inclusion of these references to other writers imply about the audience Maconie is writing for?

2 What do you think these references add to Maconie's text?

Vocabulary choices are likely to be influenced by the purpose of the text.

- Emotive vocabulary, similes and metaphors may be used to persuade or influence the reader.
- In a purely informative text, adjectives may provide factual information; in persuasive texts, they may convey opinions.
- Some texts which give advice may use a group of verbs including 'should', 'may', 'could' and 'must' (these are called **modal verbs**).
- Some texts try to establish a relationship with their readers through their use of **pronouns** – first person ('I', 'me', 'we', 'us') and second person ('you').

Look at the extract from the website Youth2Youth opposite, which offers advice to young people on a range of problems.

Activity ③

1 Decide what you think are the main purposes of this text. You should also identify the text's audience.

Now look at what one student wrote about the use of the second person pronoun 'you' in the text:

> The use of the second person pronoun throughout the text seems designed to form an intimate relationship with readers and show that the writer of the text has a sympathetic understanding of their problems. This in turn will mean readers are more likely to take on board and trust the advice being given.

This response would score highly for being analytical.

2 Write your own analytical comments about the following features of the text, exploring what effect they have and how they are suited to the audience and purpose:

   a) the frequent use of the first person plural pronouns 'our' and 'we'

   b) the use of quite sophisticated psychological vocabulary such as 'self-esteem', 'confidence', 'self image' and 'expectations'

   c) the use of vocabulary such as 'spotty' and 'bullied'.

3 Find a newspaper, magazine or online article in which you feel the writer has chosen specific items of vocabulary for effect. This might be repetition of a particular pronoun, for example, or use of very formal words. Write two to three paragraphs in which you explain the writer's reasons for the choice of at least three words.

• Sexual relationships • Self image • Emotional wellbeing • Sexuality

COMMON PROBLEMS

Self Image

You look in the mirror and you are either pleased with what you see or not. You may be looking at your physical appearance - skin, hair, clothes, or the image you portray - being confident or shy. Our self image plays an important part in how we feel about ourselves and how we think others perceive us. Our self-esteem, confidence and ability to communicate with others are closely linked with how we view ourselves.

Television, magazines and adverts tell us we live in a world full of beautiful people. The pressure to have the correct body shape, wear only branded clothes and be full of self-confidence is a tall order. Many young people compare themselves to these images and often come to the conclusion they are not meeting the standards set by the media. Thankfully most of us realise that these expectations are unrealistic. We realise that life is not like this, and how we feel about ourselves is much more important for self-esteem and confidence.

There are times however, when we are feeling down or unsure about ourselves, when we start to question our self image and don't feel as good about ourselves as we could. Sometimes this can have a spiralling negative effect and soon we feel depressed.

There are times when things can get worse. Others may comment negatively on your clothes, hair or belongings. You may be called names because you are overweight or spotty. You may even get bullied. It is these times that you are at your most vulnerable and when you look in the mirror you may start to agree with the comments. STOP. Take time out and just look carefully at the people making these comments. Are they perfect? Certainly not. Now take a look at your strengths and good qualities. Try to talk to friends about how you feel and ask them what good qualities you have. Obviously it is easier said than done but by starting to become more confident and believing in yourself, your self image will begin to improve.

Do others see you for who you really are?

Navigation sidebar

- HOME PAGE
- HELPLINE
- LIBRARY
- ABOUT US
- SUPPORTERS & LINKS
- COMMON PROBLEMS
- VOLUNTEERS

9 Understanding language choices: register

This lesson will help you to...

→ understand and describe the choice of register made in texts

→ analyse the effects of this choice

The vocabulary of a text will be chosen to suit the **audience** the text is targeted at, based on some of the things the writer assumes about them. In your controlled assessment, you will need to be able to comment on:

- the level of **formality** used in the text – whether or not it includes informal, or **colloquial** language, or even uses **slang**
- how it addresses its readers – and whether or not it uses **personal pronouns** to create a personal tone
- whether or not it uses technical or specialist language or **jargon** which it expects the audience to know – or whether the language is kept simple.

These aspects of the text are called its **register**.

Activity ❶

Read the article from the *NME* magazine about the children's TV programme *Yo Gabba Gabba!*

1 As you read, make a note of any aspects of its register and what it seems to assume about its audience.

Blimey the Kooks are looking ropey these days...

A pneumatic beat pummels with teeth-grinding 220bpm buoyancy. In the foreground a gangly twerp in a bright orange spandex baby-gro and matching furry hat flails out of time. Behind him, a warty red Cyclops, a green tri-horned monster, a pink bubble with eyes, a yellow robot and a blue cat/dragon hybrid all jiggle from side-to-side amid a Crayola landscape of green cartoon hills and salmon pink mountains. These, believe it or not, aren't the hallucinatory visions of a Dutch raver, squirming on the floor outside his aircraft hanger hoe-down at 7am. This, kiddies, is a snippet from the intro sequence to the most important children's show currently broadcasting. This is *Yo Gabba Gabba*!

2 Look at this student's comment about the opening sentence of the text:

> The range of vocabulary here is quite advanced, metaphorical and hyperbolic ('pneumatic', 'pummels', 'buoyancy') which assumes quite a literate audience willing to be entertained by creative uses of language as well as informed. The reference to 220bpm, a semi-technical abbreviation associated with dance music, also assumes a familiarity with such musical terminology.

Make comments of your own about the following details from the text:

a) This, kiddies

The writer seems to be addressing the audience as 'kiddies' – but is this article aimed at children? If not, why has the writer used this word?

b) A warty red Cyclops

You may need to look up the reference to 'Cyclops'. What does the presence of such a reference suggest about the intended audience?

c) a Crayola landscape of green cartoon hills and salmon pink mountains

Why is the reference to 'Crayola' appropriate both to the subject matter and the audience?

3 Pick out and comment on two more examples of vocabulary that suit the audience of the text.

Activity ②

1 Find two texts which have different registers. How does the register of each text suit its audience and purpose? Rewrite both of them to alter the register of the writing. You will need to think about vocabulary and sentence structure.

10 Analysing language choices: a question of grammar

This lesson will help you to...

→ understand and describe some of the grammatical choices made in texts

→ analyse the effects of these choices

Writers have to make choices about how to assemble words into sentences – what kinds of sentence (questions, statements, commands or exclamations), how long or short, how simple or complex, and how to use punctuation effectively. Grammar also influences the formality of a text; more formal texts will usually be written in **standard English**, but more informal styles may include 'non-standard' phrases from slang or regional English.

As with vocabulary, these choices are also likely to reflect the perspective, audience and purpose of the text. You will need to be able to comment on and analyse the writer's grammatical choices in your controlled assessment. For more information look at pages 82–86.

Activity 1

Read the online review of the *High School Musical* DVD which appears opposite.

1 Identify examples from the text of each of the features described in the box below.

> a) A series of one-word question-and-answer sentences (**minor sentences**).
> b) A colloquial, **non-standard** sentence.
> c) Use of **parenthesis** ( ) throughout the text.
> d) Long, extended section of text, with three linked clauses (**tricolon**).
> e) Use of **ellipsis** (…).
> f) Use of a one-word (minor sentence) **exclamation**.
> g) Use of questions, or **interrogative** sentences.
> h) Use of colloquial American English.

2 Explain in each case why you think the writer has made these choices. What is the effect of each choice?

ResultsPlus
Self assessment

Check your answer – have you:

- selected exactly the right example that is perfect for the comment you want to make?
- identified the language used by the writer?
- commented on everything the quotation has to offer you?

Activity 2

1 Identify the intended audience and the purpose of the text.

2 Look again at the features you explored in Activity 1. Organise them into two different groups using a table like the one below.

Grammatical features chosen to suit the purpose of the text	Grammatical features chosen to appeal to the text's audience

3 Use the table you have created to write two to three paragraphs to explain how the writer's choice of grammatical features are intended to appeal to the text's audience and achieve the text's purpose.

news | sport | entertainment | features | gossip

High School Musical Review

High School Musical Review

Singing? Check. Dancing? Check. Teens squealing through a musical version of high school? You got it.

What began as (I'm guessing) a made-for-the-Disney-Channel TV movie is now a DVD, perfect for those Sweet Sixteens and slumber parties where pink-clad thespians can ask who's cuter: Vanessa or Ashley, or whether Vanessa and Zac are right for each other, or who on the basketball team is the absolute dreamiest.

I needn't answer all of these tricky questions for you: you can see for yourself in *High*

Zac Efron and Vanessa Hudgens at the premiere of the film.

High School Musical Overview

★★★

OK

Rating: PG

2006

Cast and crew

Director : Kenny Ortega

Producer : Don Schain

Screenwriter : Peter Barsocchini

Starring : Zac Efron, Vanessa Anne Hudgens, Ashley Tisdale, Lucas Grabeel, Alyson Reed, Corbin Bleu, Monique Coleman, Olesya Rulin, Chris Warren Jr.

School Musical, a simple yet earnest film about the making of... a high school musical. Our lead teens Troy (Zac Efron) and Gabriella (Vanessa Anne Hudgens) are from opposite worlds but they meet at a Disneyesque vacation spot during an impromptu karaoke contest and discover, omigosh, they can both sing the daylights out of a tune.

Surprise! After summer is over, Gabriella shows up at Troy's high school (where he's best known as a basketballer, not a crooner), and they ultimately decide to tempt fate by going up for the school play. Uh oh! Trouble lurks in the form of Sharpay (Ashley Tisdale) and Ryan (Lucas Grabeel), a conceited brother-sister team who run the drama department with a teenage iron fist. Who'll win the lead? And what of the big basketball game and academic excellence contest?

You know where it's going, but *High School Musical* is surprisingly fun despite its obviousness. It helps that there are plenty of in-jokes (with a name like "Sharpay," it's gotta be good), and that the earnest cast members really want to make the film memorable. Some of the songs are appallingly bad (any of the ones that have something to do with basketball, pretty much), but for the most part it's hummably decent.

11 Analysing language choices: structure and rhetorical techniques

This lesson will help you to...

→ understand and describe some of the structural choices made in texts

→ analyse the effects of these choices

In aiming for the higher grades in your controlled assessment it is important to be able to recognise some of the special techniques used by writers to affect their audience.

Writers of texts organise their ideas in different ways to 'hook' readers in and keep them reading to the end.

- **Articles** may grab you with a 'hook' – an interesting or sensational angle on the topic – before developing the ideas in more detail.
- **Reports** will usually give us the 'who, what, where, when' in a nutshell at the start before going into more detail.
- **Advertisements** may start by suggesting a problem, or a desire, before going on to provide the solution, or fulfilment, in the form of their product.
- **Website homepages** may offer a brief, general overview of the whole site with links to pages for the detailed information.
- **Podcasts** are likely to help listeners by giving a quick summary of what the piece is about.

Activity 1

Read the opening paragraphs of an article from the magazine *games*™, given below.

1 Identify the audience and purpose(s) of the text.

2 Explain what methods the writer of the article has used to try to 'hook' in their readers.

Can Games Save Lives?

From social disaffection to high-school shootings, video games have been blamed for a lot of the world's ills. But with developers increasingly finding positive outlets for the technology, is the perception that games are bad to the bone about to change?

This year on 20 April the people of Jefferson Colorado paid their respects to the 13 people who died in one of the most shocking shootings of recent times. It has been ten years since the Columbine High School massacre, ten years since video games were unfairly implicated in the tragedy.

But in all that time very little has changed in terms of the way the medium is perceived. Sure, we have *Guitar Hero* and *Wii Fit*, but as soon as any particularly nasty youth crime is committed you can almost hear the *Daily Mail* journalists rummaging through the bins, looking for evidence that a violent FPS* was the cause of it all…

*FPS stands for 'first-person shooter' and describes games centred the use of weapons and viewed from the perspective of the player, as in the picture above.

Activity 2

Look at the text below, which is a leaflet designed to persuade readers to join the charity War on Want.

SHE'S WORKING HERSELF OUT OF POVERTY.......
YEAH, RIGHT

The fact is, she can work as hard as she likes, but unless we do something to change the way the world is organised, she'll stay poor for the rest of her days. You know that. You know that the rules are weighted in favour of developed countries. But did you know that you can do something about it, by joining War on Want?

Our starting point is that the current world order is unfair; that political and economic systems make people poor and will keep them that way. Unless we all make change happen.

That's why War on Want takes the struggle against poverty into the factories and fields as well as the corridors of power. Whilst we support local groups to join together and challenge poverty, we also highlight exploitation and injustice and call for policy changes on behalf of poor communities.

With your help we can support more anti-poverty groups, more people taking action locally and more campaigners working for political and economic change. We can make a big difference on the ground.

We'll admit our cause can be an uphill battle. But then so are most things worth fighting for. Like justice, fairness, and giving a poor woman a real chance in life.

Please join us.

1 Explain how the heading tries to create an effective opening.

2 Find a problem identified early in the text. What is the solution to the problem, according to the text?

Writers may also use a variety of rhetorical techniques to give their text impact. These include:

- the way they involve their **audience** (e.g. with the use of personal pronouns)
- the use of **emotive** language (e.g. imaginative/metaphorical language)
- different kinds of **repetition** and listing: especially in groups of three, or **triads**
- the use of **contrasts**
- the use of **rhetorical questions**
- exploiting the sounds of words (by using **alliteration**, **assonance** or **rhyme**) to create memorable phrases.

You need to be able to identify some of these and comment on their effects.

Activity 3

Re-read the War on Want leaflet above.

1 Identify examples in the text of the following features:

   a) repetition

   b) addressing the audience as 'you', then changing to 'we'

   c) repetition of key words and ideas related to poverty

   d) use of lists and contrasts

   e) metaphors and imagery related to war

   f) emotive language.

2 Now explain the effect of each of these uses of language by writing two to three sentences on each.

12 Commenting on language choices

This lesson will help you to...

→ write perceptively about language choices

You should now be ready to put what you know about language choices into practice. As when you write about images or presentation, it's not enough simply to describe the language features of a text by saying **what** devices it uses; you need to explain **how** and **why** these devices have been chosen to help you write perceptively about the texts. As you do so, it is important to use clear, precise language in your answer to the controlled assessment task, including any technical **terminology** that helps you define your points exactly.

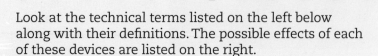

Activity  Look at the technical terms listed on the left below along with their definitions. The possible effects of each of these devices are listed on the right.

Terminology	Effect
Antithesis A pair of opposites placed together for effect in a text	• Lends emphasis to a specific contrast
Slang Informal language outside of standard English	• Affects the tone, style and register of the text, perhaps to cater to the target audience if used extensively, or to have a specific effect if used only occasionally
Second person pronoun The word 'you' (both singular and plural)	• The audience of the text is directly addressed and feels personally involved
Triad or tricolon A group of three words or phrases within a sentence	• Can be used to communicate a number of linked ideas
Connotations Associations implied by a word	• Words with the appropriate connotations suggest ideas to an audience without an extended description
Imperative A command word or phrase	• Clearly gives instructions to a reader, which sets an authoritative tone

1 Find an example of a text which uses one or more of the above devices and explain the effect it creates within the text, ensuring you use the technical terminology correctly.

2 Now select the appropriate terms to describe the techniques used in each of the following sentences:

a) Take the dog for a walk!

b) It was a very dark night: the fog was thick; the moon was bright but covered in cloud; the branches of the trees crowded densely overhead.

c) He was lying on the beach while in the UK it was raining.

Activity ❷

Read the article below from *FourFourTwo* magazine about the difficulties faced by young footballers trying to make the grade with a professional club.

1 Begin by noting down the main ideas of the article, its purpose(s) and audience.

2 Next identify some of the significant language choices in the text (vocabulary, grammar, structure, rhetoric) and make further notes on the effect of these in preparation for a more extended piece of writing about this text.

Some interesting features for comment have been highlighted and some prompts provided to get you started.

Vocabulary: Explain the effect of the 'cattle market' metaphor.

Structure: Comment on the way the headline and standfirst lead into the text.

TERROR

The exit trials are football's cattle market – one last chance for rejected youngsters to save their career. FFT meets up with three players who know that one bad game and it's all over.

Grammar/ structure: Comment on the impact of the short opening sentence. How does it produce a 'twist', when we reach the second paragraph?

It must be the biggest haul of silverware in the whole of Essex. Taylor Sinfield's lavish front room is a shrine to athletic achievement, with cupboards full of trophies, drawers stuffed with medals and shelves creaking under shiny figurines.

Rhetoric: How does the writer use antithesis in the second paragraph?

Sadly, most of them aren't his. The Sinfields of Canvey Island are a famous sporting name alright, but it's Taylor's judo-champion sisters who've been making the headlines from local to international level. He, on the other hand has just been given the boot by Charlton Athletic, and now faces the season's most harrowing match: the exit trial, a sort of footballing cattle market, as teams of recently rejected young players desperately try to catch a scout's eye and salvage their career.

'Being a footballer is everything to me at the moment,' says the 18-year-old, gazing at those trophies from the dining room table. 'I've got a back-up plan, but I just hope someone takes a chance on me.'

Structure: Comment on the effect of the alternation of reporting and direct quotation.

Behind him, mum Sharon is wringing her hands nervously. 'I'm not going tomorrow,' she says. 'I don't want to put him on edge. His dad always goes. I'm here to pick up the pieces.'

Vocabulary: How do the highlighted words create contrast? Look at 'harrowing' and 'desperately'. Comment on the emotive language here and the suitability of 'given the boot'.

Last-chance saloon

Summer is an anxious time for young footballers. While your Michael Owens are running down their contracts to secure lucrative deals elsewhere, a great swathe of hopefuls are failing to become players in the first place. In the Football League around 60% of apprentices are released before turning pro, with up to 95% then leaving the game by the age of 21. The exit trial is a cruel but necessary follow-up to that initial rejection, and *FourFourTwo* has a front-row seat as three recent discards prepare to parade their skills at the last-chance saloon: Brentford's Griffin Park.

Vocabulary: Comment on how the highlighted words create a sense of emotional drama and tension.

Once you have picked out some interesting language features in the *FourFourTwo* magazine article, you need to get your ideas down clearly and accurately.

Activity 3

1   Select four of the significant points you have noted about the text and create a paragraph about each point which follows the pattern shown below:

State the point clearly in a single, well-constructed sentence. This is the topic sentence for the paragraph.

> The vocabulary in this text includes some fairly emotive language. For example, it uses the metaphor 'football's cattle market' to describe the exit trial. This implies that the young players are not being treated as human beings but as animals to be bought and sold without any feeling, and so conveys the writer's disapproval.

Refer specifically to an example from the text and use the relevant terminology.

The vital bit – say how, or why, or with what effect this vocabulary is used.

2   Now write an introductory paragraph and a concluding paragraph for your piece of writing on the article in which you comment on the overall effectiveness of the text.

Assessment practice

As part of your controlled assessment task you could explore how the writers communicate their ideas and perspectives using language.

Activity 4

First identify both the audience and purpose of the website opposite. Then write a response to this question:

How does Eurotrip use languages to communicate its ideas and perspectives?

You should spend 10 minutes on this task.

ResultsPlus
Self assessment

Before you complete this self-assessment activity, you might like to read some sample answers to this task on the following pages (44 – 45).

1 Check your answer to Activity 4:

- Did you select quotations from the text that perfectly summed up what the text was about?
- Did you identify the language used and confidently use the relevant terminology in your comment?
- Did you link the writer's use of language to their ideas and perspective, considering the intended impact on the reader?

2 Now decide which Band your answer to Activity 4 falls into by applying the mark scheme to the right. You will need to be careful and precise in your marking.

■ **Band 3**

- selects quotations to comment on and clearly links the examples to the points being made
- comments on language are sound and show the point being developed
- makes clear links between the language used and the writer's ideas and perspectives

● **Band 4**

- selects small parts of the quotations (perhaps one word or a sentence) to focus on in detail
- comments on language are detailed
- makes thorough comments on the links between the language used and the writer's ideas and perspectives

▲ **Band 5**

- selects well-chosen examples that fully support the point being made
- comments on language are perceptive
- perceptive exploration of the ideas and perspectives of the writer

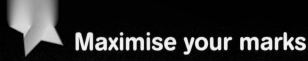

How does Eurotrip use language to communicate its ideas and perspectives?

Here are three student answers to the language task on page 42. Read the answers together with the examiner comments around and after the answers. Then complete the activity at the bottom of page 45.

Student 1 – Extract typical of a grade B answer

The comment on the imperative and personal pronoun are connected to one point in the text, showing analysis of the ideas and perspectives.

Eurotrip uses some factual language when it says "With over 17,000 registered users" and this makes the reader realise that it's a good site if so many people use it, people want to be part of a large group. The site also uses instructive language when it uses the command "Click a city. Find a hostel" — the imperative "click" clearly tells the reader what to do. This is because the site aims to appear helpful and caring, shown when it says "If you … want help finding cheap airfares." The use of the personal pronoun "you" means the reader feels like the site cares for their needs individually.

The quotation selected is the appropriate part of the text that the student then comments on.

Some detail to support the comment on why the website mentioned the number of users.

Examiner summary

This part of the answer is typical of a grade B performance. This student selects the appropriate part of a sentence to explore factual language and its use. The student has thought carefully about their point on the audience and states that they want to feel like a large group. The student's response is particularly strong when it connects the imperative and the personal pronoun and explores the idea of the reader needing to feel cared for.

Student 2 – Extract typical of a grade A answer

Confident use of language terminology, while showing understanding of the term.

The language on the homepage of the website is purposefully concise, using imperatives to tell the reader what to do with 'click' and 'find a hostel'. The page is designed to communicate what the whole site is about and to persuade the reader to use the service. Such imperatives serve to persuade the reader as the phrases tell the reader what to do. However, the use of adjectives in the description of the places makes the site more persuasive with 'beautiful', 'massive' and 'quintessential'. These words make the places seem amazing and will inspire the reader to plan their trip.

A development of the idea using appropriate examples to support the point made.

Examiner summary

This part of the answer is typical of a grade A performance. The student has developed an idea about the main point of view in the site and selected examples to fully support the idea. The examples are a little obvious and don't show the discrimination of the top grade.

Identifies the effect as well as the types of word used, with brief examples.

The aim of the site is to persuade the reader to continue into the main site and use the services of the company. There is an obvious use of exaggeration in the adjectives selected with 'massive' and 'quintessential' that serves to excite the reader to the possibilities of the trips. More interesting is the use of paradox in the descriptions that appeal to the audience of the site. With the idea of 'beautiful architecture' comes the idea of 'unbridled debauchery' and with 'quaint attitude' comes 'raucous soul'. The site is clearly aimed at young travellers who might appreciate culture but would also be interested in partying.

Selection of advanced terminology with examples and analysis of the reasons for this language choice.

Examiner summary

This part of the answer is typical of a grade A* performance. The student has chosen to write about paradox as opposed to imperatives and this shows more sophistication. This is a well-developed point focusing on the audience and purpose of the website. Quotations support the idea of the varied interests of the audience.

Results**Plus**
Build better answers

Move from a Grade (B) to Grade (A)

In this part of the task you need to follow ideas up. You should try to use different examples to expand on the same idea within a paragraph rather than listing lots of techniques that cover a variety of ideas. Student 1 does show an understanding of language but Student 2 is more successful because they stay focused on the idea of persuasion.

Aim for a Grade (A*)

In this part of the task you need to select quotations and use language terms that show your understanding. Student 2 selects good quotations and uses language terms confidently but Student 3 shows further understanding by effectively analysing a more complex feature of the text.

Putting it into practice

1 Take a sentence from a text such as a newspaper headline or advert slogan. Consider why each word was selected and how it is used by the writer to suit audience and purpose.

13 Selecting examples

This lesson will help you to...

→ **select examples to support the points you make about a text**

→ **include quotations effectively in your writing**

When you are writing your controlled assessment response, it is vital that you refer in detail to the texts and include examples which you quote. Your examples are your evidence, and you will gain high marks for the skilful and relevant use of quotations.

Some techniques for introducing quotations are illustrated below, referring to the well-known nursery rhyme 'Jack and Jill'.

1   Use **parentheses** (brackets) and **ellipses** (...) for brief, passing quotations:

> In 'Jack and Jill', the use of repeated verbs with violent connotations ('fell down'... 'broke'...'tumbling') help convey the dramatic nature of Jack and Jill's fall.

2   Introduce and explain a quotation, putting it in context and using a **colon** (:):

> According to the text, the medical treatment Jack received was somewhat unorthodox: 'He went to bed and bound his head
> With vinegar and brown paper.'

3   Integrate the quotation into your sentence. This is called **integrated referencing** and is very useful for shorter quotations and for commenting on language choices. You may have to edit the quotation and show this using **brackets**:

> How serious was Jack's injury? The text suggests that Jack 'broke his crown' but goes on to note that he 'trot(ed)' home afterwards 'as fast as he could caper'. The verbs 'trot' and 'caper' both imply a certain lightness of foot and energy not entirely compatible with a fractured skull.

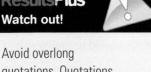

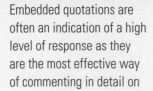

Activity ❶

Read the text opposite which is a blog from *Empire* magazine written by the journalist Chris Hewitt.

1   **Identify the purpose of the writing. Which of the following quotations from the text would be best to use in an explanation of this purpose?**

   A   '...the Oscars' Best Picture race will include ten nominees, rather than the traditional five...'

   B   '...a largely cynical move to acknowledge films that don't have a chance of scooping the big prize.'

   C   'It's a decision that has split pundits down the middle.'

10 Oscar Nominees Per Year?

posted on Thursday June 25, 2009, 09:58 by Chris Hewitt

So, as of next year, the Oscars' Best Picture race will include ten nominees, rather than the traditional five, the biggest sea change for the ceremony since the minting of the Best Animated Feature Film category (ironically, a category that may be threatened by this new move; more on that later). It's a decision that has split pundits down the middle. Everyone's favourite grumpy old man, Jeff Wells over at Hollywood Elsewhere, has bah-humbugged the whole enterprise – "Why didn't the Academy decide to nominate 15 films for Best Picture?" he asks – while Steven Zeitchick at The Hollywood Reporter thinks it's a potentially positive move, calling it a "shrewd marketing move" even if it's also "a questionable policy change."

Meanwhile, in my initial spur-of-the-moment reaction in our news story, I pooh-poohed the idea, seeing it as a largely cynical move to acknowledge films that don't have a chance of scooping the big prize. And I still stand by that – largely. It's pretty apparent that the Academy decided to do this, not to return the Oscars to their heyday (the last time more than five films completed for the li'l golden guy was in 1943, back when Hitler had no idea that he would become a YouTube punchline), but because of the criticism that came its way in the wake of the shocking snub handed out to the likes of **The Dark Knight, Gran Torino, Wall-E** and **Eagle Eye**, four films which were demonstrably better than actual Best Picture nominee, **The Reader**.

Empire Blog RSS Feed

CATEGORIES

London Film Festival 2009

Words From The Wise

The Empire Blog

Comic-Con Diaries

RECENT POSTS

Finally! Demos's LFF round-up...
By Damon Wise

Help Avert World War III
By Helen O'Hara

How Scary Should Kids Movies Be?
By Helen O'Hara

Videobiogisode Day 16
By Chris Hewitt

Who Should Host The Oscars Now?
By Helen O'Hara

Videobiogisode Day 15
By Chris Hewitt

Videobiogisode Day 14
By Chris Hewitt

Videobiogisode Day 13
By Chris Hewitt

Activity 2

1 Imagine you have been asked to write about the way the writer conveys his perspective. For each of the features of the text listed below, select a relevant quotation and use it to construct a paragraph which explains the effect given.

   a) The writer's use of slang ➜ conveys his light-hearted attitude towards the controversy.

   b) Use of a rhetorical question ➜ conveys scepticism about the change.

   c) Use of long complex sentences including parentheses ➜ allows the writer to fully explain his perspective on events.

   d) Use of quotations ➜ shows how the writer is efficiently summarising both sides of the debate.

14 Comparing texts

This lesson will help you to...

→ make effective comparisons between two texts

Making an effective comparison between two texts is possibly the most challenging aspect of this unit, and it is a skill which you will need to master if you are to achieve the highest grades. The mark scheme talks about making 'discriminating comparisons showing insight' which involves thinking about two texts at the same time, pointing out interesting similarities and differences and bringing together supporting examples or quotations, a process sometimes referred to as **collating**.

Activity ❶

To explore the techniques involved, imagine you have been asked to compare not two texts but two celebrity footballers or actors. You can choose your own, but as an example let's take the footballers Wayne Rooney and Cristiano Ronaldo.

1 Note any points you would include in the comparison – some have been suggested below.

Rooney in 2010	Ronaldo in 2010
Forward player; frequent goalscorer	Also a forward – more of a winger. Also a frequent goalscorer
Powerful and strong	Different style of player; skilful dribbler, famous for spectacular free kicks
Has played for Everton, Manchester United and England	Has also played for Manchester United as well as Sporting Lisbon, Real Madrid and Portugal

Below is the opening paragraph for an extended piece of writing which compares and contrasts Rooney with Ronaldo:

> Both Rooney and Ronaldo are highly talented international forwards, and in many ways we can see similarities between them. However, there are also significant differences in terms of their careers, personalities and nationality.

2 Now write a paragraph of your own which follows on from this opening and which focuses on a particular point of comparison or contrast, backing up your point with examples as far as possible.

3   Go on to write a full comparison either of Rooney and Ronaldo, or of two celebrities of your choice, making sure that in each paragraph you make a comparison or a contrast between them. Highlight the comparisons and contrasts you make by using the following connecting words and phrases effectively:

Making a comparison	Making a contrast
Both Rooney and Ronaldo…	Rooney… **By contrast**, Ronaldo…
Rooney and Ronaldo **have this much in common**…	**Whereas** Rooney… Ronaldo…
In the case of Rooney… **Similarly**, Ronaldo…	Rooney… **On the other hand**, Ronaldo…
Rooney is… **Likewise**, Ronaldo…	**Unlike** Rooney, who…, Ronaldo…
	Ronaldo is… This is **quite different from** Rooney, who…

In your controlled assessment you will be asked to compare two texts on the same theme. You will need to think about the different ideas and perspectives of the two texts, and this will include looking at language and presentational devices.

Look at the two texts on pages 54 and 55. They are part of a sample controlled assessment-style question. The first is an article from *The Times*, and the second is a page from the website of Greenpeace, an environmental organisation. Both these texts are on the theme of climate change. The question you will be answering is:

Compare these two texts on the theme of climate change. Explore how the writers communicate their ideas and perspectives.

First of all, you could think about each of the texts in turn and identify similarities and differences as you do this.

Activity ②

1   Create a table like the one below across a page.

2   As you study the two texts in turn, work downwards, making notes and adding quotes from each text in the appropriate boxes in preparation for a more extended piece of writing in which you compare the two texts.

	Greenpeace website	*The Times* article
Audience and purpose		
Overview of ideas and perspectives		
Presentational devices		
Language choices		

You will need to plan how you are going to compare the two texts, so that when you write your response to the task you are able to embed comparison throughout your writing.

Activity 3

1 Plan the structure of your answer by making notes on the similarities and differences between the two texts on pages 54 and 55. You might find it helpful to work across the table of notes you made in Activity 2, exploring each category for comparison in turn. Below is an example of one student's planning for their opening paragraph, focusing on an overview of the two texts' audiences and purposes.

	Similarities	Differences
Audience and purpose	Both persuade readers that they can/should take action. Both include some alarming information to shock readers. Both present a problem and go on to offer a solution.	The Greenpeace webpage uses 'we' throughout to create a sense of togetherness, but the first person use in *The Times* article makes it a personal viewpoint. Greenpeace website — already sympathetic? Times readers — more conservative? Greenpeace webpage seems to want dramatic, even political, action from its readers but the Times is less drastic. Greenpeace expects its audience to completely change lifestyle, but the Times suggests smaller changes may be enough.

Read the following paragraph. It is the opening of one student's response to the sample controlled assessment task and is based on the plan above.

Both texts have similar purposes and audiences. They both begin by reminding their readers of the seriousness of the problem (by including some shocking facts and statistics in the Greenpeace webpage and the reference to the melting ice in *The Times*) and go on to persuade their readers that they can and should do something about it. Both of them suggest that there is a possible solution which their readers can actively contribute towards. However, in other ways they are quite different. The readers of a Greenpeace website may already be sympathetic to the environmental point of view that a radical change in lifestyle might be needed, and the repeated use of the first person plural 'we' suggests they are all in this together. The writer of the *Times* article, however, uses the first person singular 'I' to offer a personal viewpoint and reassures the more conservative readers of the newspaper that some small changes may be enough.

ResultsPlus

Build better answers

Look at this part of a controlled assessment task:

Your task is to compare the material on two texts.

■ A Band 3 answer will have **sound comparisons** of image, presentation and language throughout the answer. However, it may deal with each text separately.

● A Band 4 answer will include **specific and detailed comparisons** of two texts, with detailed comments on image, presentation and language throughout the answer. The selection of examples included will be detailed and appropriate, and will support the points being made.

▲ A Band 5 answer will make **discriminating comparisons**, selecting only those aspects of image, presentation and language that allow perceptive comments. These comparisons will be littered throughout the text.

2 Think about ways in which this could be improved by adding quotations and further details, or by altering wording or punctuation.

3 Now complete the full response to the sample controlled assessment task, using your planning from Question 1.

Activity 4

1 Look at the poster below. Write a response to the same sample controlled assessment task given on page 49, comparing this text and the Greenpeace webpage on page 55. This time you should focus particularly on the use of images.

Controlled assessment practice

Examiner's tip

This is a sample Unit 1 controlled assessment for GCSE English and GCSE English Language.

Examiner's tip

Your controlled assessment task will be based on a theme. All the questions and texts will focus on that theme.

Examiner's tip

These are the texts provided by Edexcel. You must pick two of these texts.

Turn to page 54 to see two of these texts, or to see all six texts visit www.edexcel.com.

Examiner's tip

1000 words might not seem like enough but remember that Band 5 mentions words such as 'discrimination', and emphasises that you should focus on well-chosen ideas. Be concise in order to get the highest grade.

Guidance for students: Reading/Studying Written Language (Reading) Task

What do I have to do?
You will complete one reading/studying written language (reading) task on the theme of the environment.

You must complete this task on your own.

How much time do I have?
Following your preparation, you will have up to two hours to complete the task.

How do I prepare for the task?
For the chosen theme:
- select **two** texts from the Edexcel texts provided
- prepare by making notes and planning your response to the task.

Environment texts

1 *Guardian* podcast	2 Aeroplanes and Global Warming article
3 Greenpeace climate change webpage*	4 *Your Environment* magazine cover
5 The Great Global Warming Swindle trailer	6 *The Times* article on air travel*

What must my response to the task show?
The response must show that you can:
- make comparisons between two environment texts
- select appropriate details from two environment texts to support your ideas
- explore how writers use images, presentation and language to communicate their ideas and perspectives in two environment texts.

How should I present my response?
A written response of up to 1000 words.

The Reading/Studying Written Language (Reading) Task for the student

Your task is to compare the material from **two** texts on the environment.

In your comparison you must:
- explore how the writers communicate their ideas and perspectives
- comment on how the writers use presentation and language
- include examples to illustrate the points you make.

Examiner's tip

Focus your response on the writer's ideas and perspectives and use examples of presentation and language to support your points.

Here are two of the texts provided for this task:

'You don't need to forsake your
fun in the sun to help combat
climate change'
Jane Knight, *The Times*,
17 November 2007

You don't need to forsake your fun in the sun to help combat climate change

Going green isn't just about the number of flights you make, it's also the type of holiday you choose and how you behave on it.

Jane Knight: *Deputy Travel Editor*

What's to be done? In the week that the UN Secretary General Ban Ki Moon visited Antarctica to be told that an ice sheet covering a fifth of the continent may crumble, we also hear that more travellers are balking at spending extra on holidays to help curb climate change.

And who can blame them? If dinner-table chatter is anything to go by, my friends are sick of hearing that they should forsake their fun in the sun to reduce their carbon footprint. No one wants to feel guilty about taking those well-earned holidays. And why should they, asks a colleague pointedly, when livestock generates more harmful emissions through – er – excessive flatulence than aircraft do?

Already faced with hefty fuel surcharges, passengers are reluctant to shell out more, even if it does help the environment. A study by the travel industry marketing specialist BLM Media showed that 35 per cent of respondents would not pay an extra £20 a holiday to offset carbon emissions, while an even greater 59 per cent would not cut down on the number of times they go abroad. Which is why Qatar Airways' announcement this week that it aims to be the first airline to be powered by a gas-based fuel could be revolutionary. It may not happen – an in-depth study is first needed – but at least this shows that airlines are doing something more than passing the green buck on to passengers. Virgin Atlantic has already announced plans to run a plane on biofuel next year.

Going green, though, isn't just about cutting the number of flights you make or offsetting your carbon emissions. It's also about the type of holiday you choose and how you behave on it. I've lost count of the number of hotels that trumpet their "green" credentials by encouraging you to recycle your bath towels, then change your towels twice daily anyway. I prefer to stay in small lodges or hotels where locals form part of the workforce and where hoteliers become involved in the local community, the kind of place you'll find on the useful website responsibletravel.com.

Eco-tourism doesn't have to be the oxymoron that the wildlife advocate Richard Leakey says it is. But as he points out in this issue, it does need international standards. We know how environmentally friendly washing machines are when we buy them, so why can't tourism be rated in a similar way?

Above all, responsible tourism is about awareness, not necessarily at increased cost. Ten years ago, recycling your rubbish in England was almost unheard of. What we need today is a similar change in attitude towards how we holiday.

The message is starting to trickle through. Just minutes after the New Forest this week took three accolades in the Virgin Holidays Responsible Tourism Awards, organised by Responsibletravel.com, Jamaica's tourism chiefs invited the man behind it all to their country, so they could benefit from his wisdom. Responsible tourism doesn't have to cost more, and it doesn't mean we have to stop travelling, but if we want our children, and our children's children, to benefit from travel as we do, we need to start thinking in a slightly deeper shade of green.

Climate change webpage
Greenpeace UK

http://www.greenpeace.org.uk/climate

GREENPEACE UK

Donate | Take action | Sign up for email

Home | Blog | About Greenpeace | **What we do**

▼ Climate change
The problems
The solutions
What we are doing
What you can do
Videos
Related links

▶ Forests
▶ Oceans
▶ Nuclear power
▶ Peace
▶ GM food
▶ Toxic chemicals

What you can do
Donate now
Community
Media centre

Search [ ] Go

Log in | Register

RSS | What is RSS?

GP Worldwide

Home > What we do

Climate change

The world is warming up. Already 150,000 people are dying every year because of climate change and, within 50 years, one-third of all land-based species could face extinction. If we carry on the way we are now, by 2100 the planet will likely be hotter than it's been at any point in the past two million years.

But catastrophic climate change isn't inevitable. We know that climate change is caused by burning fossil fuels. The technologies that could dramatically reduce our dependence on fossil fuels – **decentralised energy**, **renewables** and **efficiency**, hybrid cars, efficient buildings – already exist and have been proven to work. If we start cutting our emissions now, using these ready-to-go technologies, then there is still a chance to avoid the most catastrophic impacts of climate change.

What we're lacking is real action. The government needs to put in place meaningful policies to urgently reduce emissions – and to act on them immediately. Under New Labour, carbon emissions have risen. The government is set to miss its own emissions targets. Whether through political cowardice or industry lobbying, the government is failing to put their words into action.

We're the last generation that can stop this global catastrophe, and we need your help.

TAKE ACTION | **The problems** | **The solutions**

Airplot - the plot to stop airport expansion

We've bought a plot of land on the proposed third runway site at Heathrow. Sign up to get your piece of the plot and help stop airport expansion.

more » | support us »

Copenhagen photo exhibition illustrates extent of climate change »

GREENPEACE GIVING gifts to change the world!

Watch Coalfinger

Watch our 007 spoof Coalfinger and share it with your friends to spread the word about the menace of coal.

Climate news

- Copenhagen photo exhibition illustrates extent of climate change
- 1 minute to save the world - and the winner is...
- Join the Youth Climate Coalition in a worldwide call for a Real Deal at Copenhagen!
- Tuvalu stops play in Copenhagen by demanding legally-binding agreement
- Place your bets for the Copenhagen Fossil Of The Day

more »

55

Unit 1 English Today: Writing

This section of the book will help you to develop your writing skills, exploring how to write for different audiences and purposes, and to express your ideas clearly and precisely. The texts and activities in this unit will help you develop the skills you need to generate ideas for your writing task, plan it effectively and to structure and craft your writing by using engaging vocabulary and sentences, all of which will help you to achieve the best grade that you can in your Unit 1 controlled assessment task

Your assessment

This unit is a controlled assessment unit. You will complete one writing task which you will have two hours to complete. You can write up to 1000 words. You will be asked to complete one task from a choice of two, which will be linked to the theme of your reading task in this unit. You will have had the chance to look at the task and make notes to plan your response in advance so that you feel prepared to complete this part of the controlled assessment.

Your response to the task must show that you can:

✔ make choices in your writing that are appropriate to the audience and purpose

✔ make sure that you spell, punctuate and use grammar accurately and appropriately for the purpose of your writing and to achieve the desired effect.

Assessment Objectives

Your response to the writing task will be marked using these Assessment Objectives:

✔ Write clearly, effectively and imaginatively, using and adapting forms and selecting vocabulary appropriate to the task and purpose in ways that engage the reader

✔ Organise information and ideas into structured and sequenced sentences, paragraphs and whole texts, using a variety of linguistic and structural features to support cohesion and overall coherence.

✔ Use a range of sentence structures for clarity, purpose and effect, with accurate punctuation and spelling.

This student book unit will help you to understand what these require you to do so that you can write a successful response to your controlled assessment writing task.

1 Writing with purpose: to inform, explain and review

Your controlled assessment writing task will make its primary purpose clear. In this lesson we will focus on writing to inform, explain, or review.

The primary purpose given in your controlled assessment task will be a major factor in deciding not just what you write, but how you write it. However, you may need to use other kinds of writing to support this primary purpose. For example, in a review of a concert you will need to use some facts to inform the reader about the concert and describe some elements of it to support the opinions you express.

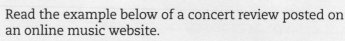

Activity ❶

Read the example below of a concert review posted on an online music website.

---

music **OMH**

home / film / theatre / classical / music

MUSIC: gig reviews

blog / features / reviews: festivals / gigs / albums

Kaiser Chiefs ★★★★★

Carling Live 24 @ Brixton Academy, London, 28 April 2006

"What do ya reckon the 'K' and the 'C' stand for, mate?" asked the innocent bystander, staring at the huge gold-embossed initials on the stage curtain and clearly unaware of the incendiary indie about to be unleashed upon a slightly subdued Academy crowd.

The promise of music, a whole day's worth, lured an eclectic crowd to Brixton Academy for an early evening start to a third year of successive gigs and parties over 24 hours.

With the Kaiser Chiefs scheduled for a 9.15pm start, The Pipettes and Captain supported admirably but probably felt under-appreciated as the crowd milled between bar and stage showing only a passing interest in choreographed hand dancing from three girls in spotty dresses and the more sombre, grander sound of Captain. Both provided an interesting musical juxtaposition to the Kaiser Chiefs' explosive start which finally shook the crowd awake.

Expertly wielding a cow bell or tambourine throughout, Ricky Wilson jumped and cavorted his way over every inch of the stage reeling off crowd-friendly tracks from Employment and introducing three new tracks (Learnt My Lesson Well, High Royds and Heart Dies Down) by declaring "We are Kaiser Chiefs and we're planning on being Kaiser Chiefs for a little while." This is no bad thing, if the quality of this new material is anything to go by.

You Can Have It All was particularly memorable for one blushing crowd member as she was hoisted up on stage to perform a slightly stilted ballroom dance routine with Ricky Wilson, who also popped up on the mixing desk stage for part of I Predict A Riot before haring it back on stage for a livewire finale to a thoroughly enjoyable gig.

1　The primary purpose of this text is to review. Which of the following writing purposes are also used in the text to support this primary purpose? Identify examples from the text to support your answer.

　　A Writing to inform　　　　　　**B** Writing to explain

　　C Writing to describe　　　　　**D** Writing to entertain

2　For each secondary writing purpose you identified, write a sentence or two explaining why you think the writer used them.

Most writing tasks will need you to convey some sort of information which could be statistics, quotes from experts, or background information. If your purpose is to explain, you need to give more support so that your audience will understand your information without further help.

Activity 2

Think about what you would need to do if you were writing a review of a new feature film.

1 Put in rank order the following sorts of information according to which will be the most important (1) and the least important (5) to include in your response:

- Facts and statistics about your topic
- Quotes from relevant experts
- Evidence from your personal experience
- Opinions about the topic from other people
- Background information such as biographical details

When you are writing to review, the information, explanation or description you give should support the most important feature: your opinion.

Activity 3

Look again at the review of the Kaiser Chiefs' concert, particularly focusing on use of information and description.

1 How would you sum up the writer's opinion of this concert in one word? Explain why you have chosen this word.

2 Identify one piece of information or description which you feel helps the reader understand the writer's opinion. Write a sentence or two explaining your answer.

3 Identify one piece of information or description which you feel does not help the reader understand the writer's opinion. Write a sentence or two explaining your answer.

Activity 4

Look at the following controlled assessment writing task:

> Write a review of a feature film you have seen recently for a website aimed at teenagers.

1 Write the opening three paragraphs of your feature film review, thinking about how you will communicate your opinion using information and description.

2 Writing with purpose: to influence, advise, persuade and argue

This lesson will help you to...

→ make effective choices when writing to influence, advise, persuade and argue

Many writing tasks involve trying to influence or persuade your audience in some way. To convince them of your point of view, you need to think carefully about what you say and how you say it.

In this lesson we will focus on writing a well-reasoned argument with a series of logically connected ideas, supported by evidence, that leads to a conclusion. Put simply, it means **making a case** for something. Your writing task will involve constructing an argument if you need to:

- influence readers to accept your opinion
- advise readers in some way
- sell readers something
- persuade readers to do something.

Activity ①

Look at the article opposite from an online football forum.

1 Write down:

a) the purpose(s) of the text

b) the audience of the text

c) the tone and register of the writing

d) the conclusion which the writer wants his audience to arrive at.

Using some of the following **persuasive techniques** in your writing is likely to help your argument achieve its desired effect:

directly addressing your readers

lists

contrasts and sets of opposites (antithesis)

exaggeration, or hyperbole

rhetorical questions

similes, metaphors and comparisons

sound patterns such as alliteration and assonance

irony

Activity ②

Look again at the text from the football forum webpage.

1 Identify examples of the persuasive techniques above.

2 Write a sentence for each technique you find to explain the effect it has on the audience of the text.

FOOTBALL

Home | News | Match Centre | **Opinion** | Archive | World Cup | Pictures | Premier League | Championship | More Clubs

Home | Opinion | Columnists | Ian Winwood

Why the unfair Premier League must either introduce a salary cap, or force the big five's players to drink Guinness at half-time

By Ian Winwood

It has become a bit fashionable to bang on about how unfair the Premier League is. As we all know, it is a league whose odds are stacked in favour not just of 'big clubs' but of any club with a great deal of money. Millionaire owners are these days considered paupers. If your club isn't the play-thing of a billionaire, you're no longer in the game.

But fear not, because I've figured out a solution, a way of making the league much fairer for its poorer clubs. It comes in the form of a handicap system, and here's how it works.

Any match where Manchester United, Arsenal, Liverpool, Chelsea or Manchester City are playing any other team in the Premier League, the system of rewards will change. Because these big clubs are expected to win, a greater incentive than mere points must be put in place for their opponents. These are as follows.

1) If any of the big five clubs are beaten by a team who last season played in the Championship, the winning team will be awarded 10 points.

2) If this victory comes on the road, the losing manager will be forced to wear a clown suit on the touchline for the next three matches.

3) When any of the big five clubs play teams outside of their own elite circle, their opponents will be awarded a one goal start. If the game is an away match for the smaller team, each player on the home team will be forced to drink one pint of lager for each goal they score.

4) No matter their opponents, each player fielded by the big five clubs must eat a full English breakfast – including chips and black pudding – twenty five minutes before the start of each game. At half time they must drink two pints of Guinness and one kilogram of marzipan.

5) Each time the big five play away from home, they must travel to their opponent's ground using public transport. Should they lose the match, they must hitchhike home.

6) Come season's end, if any one of the big five clubs finishes outside of the top five places in the Premier League, they will be relegated. Not to the Championship, but the Scottish League Division 2.

7) Failure by any one of the big five clubs to win any trophy that season will result in the team's chairman spending the next season in prison.

I'm sure you'll agree that these changes to the established way of doing things are both sensible and fair, and will only add to the quality and entertainment on offer in 'The Best League In The World.' In fact, I expect my ideas to be warmly embraced by the big cheeses and the FA, and implemented at the start of next season.

There is, though, an even simpler way of lessening the distance between those that have and those that don't have anywhere near as much. It's called a salary cap, and if one isn't implemented soon then football is likely to get even further out of control than it already is.

And where's the sport in that?

An argument need not be even-handed; ultimately it might take sides – but a skilfully constructed argument will anticipate what 'the other side' might say and include this **counter-argument** in order to reject or dismiss it.

You can do this by using phrases like these:

Some people might argue that…	However…
It is sometimes said that…	This is far from the case because…

It helps your readers to follow your thinking if you flag up the logic of your case by using appropriate **connectives**:

Adding more reasons	Leading towards conclusions
Not only… but also In addition… Furthermore… Moreover…	So… Therefore… It follows from this that… Inevitably…

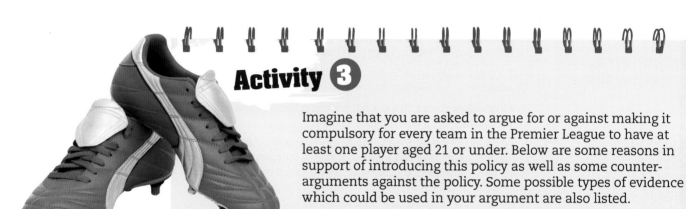

Activity ❸

Imagine that you are asked to argue for or against making it compulsory for every team in the Premier League to have at least one player aged 21 or under. Below are some reasons in support of introducing this policy as well as some counter-arguments against the policy. Some possible types of evidence which could be used in your argument are also listed.

Reasons in support of the policy	Counter-arguments against the policy	Possible evidence to draw on
Hard for young players to come through the ranks	Discriminates against older players	Numbers of players aged 21 or under in Premier League
Would increase diversity within teams	Younger players are less experienced and more risky for teams	Information about the training received by young players and the try-out process
Would ensure new talent could flourish and maintain the high standards of football we enjoy	There may not be any young players who are good enough to play in the Premier League	Opinions of supporters, managers or other experts
		Career histories of both successful players and examples of less successful players

1 Use this information to help you write four to five paragraphs of an argument, either for or against the policy, using appropriate connectives and persuasive techniques.

Activity 4

Now think about the following controlled assessment writing task:

> Write an article for a teenagers' website in which you persuade your readers to take part in more of the sports activities on offer in your local area.

1   In what ways will it involve making a case? Make notes on the following questions:

  a) What is your conclusion? What do you want your readers to think, feel or do after reading your text?

  b) What are the main ideas or reasons you will offer to help you achieve this effect on readers?

  c) What kinds of evidence would be convincing? These might include facts, figures and examples.

  d) Which aspect(s) of the counter-argument might you include, and how will you reject this line of argument?

2   Write a conclusion to your article in which you sum up your argument and the evidence you have used to support this.

3 Writing for your audience: content

This lesson will help you to...

→ decide what to include in your writing according to your audience

Your controlled assessment writing task will tell you something about the **audience** you are writing for, and you will be assessed partly according to how well you have taken this into account in your writing. Accurately identifying the target audience from the task will help you decide not just what to write but how to write it.

Activity ①

Look at this example of a controlled assessment writing task:

> Write an article for an online magazine for teenage girls about the use of size zero models in fashion shows and advertising.

Answer the following questions to plan what and how you would need to write for this audience.

1 Is the audience defined by age, gender or occupation?
2 What should you assume about the interests and attitudes of your readers?
3 How hard do you think you will need to try to interest them in your topic?
4 Why might your readers either want, or need, to know what you have to tell them?
5 How much do you think they already know and understand about the topic?

Results Plus
Controlled assessment tip

Ask yourself the questions on the right about your own controlled assessment task before you start planning.

The way you have answered these questions about your audience and what you can assume about them will largely decide what kind of material you will include in your writing. The next step is to decide what type of content you need to include to appeal to your audience.

Activity ②

1 Put in rank order the following types of material for the audience of the task in Activity 1, with 1 being the most important and 6 being the least important:

- **Quotes and studies** from psychological experts about the influence of fashion on girls' body image.
- News **reports** that some fashion shows will no longer be using 'size zero' models.
- **Case studies** of individual girls who have suffered eating disorders.
- **Interviews** with models who work in the fashion industry.
- **Facts and statistics** about numbers of young people suffering from eating disorders.
- **Personal opinion** and/or experience.

E

Activity 3

Look at this example of a controlled assessment writing task:

> Write an article for an online magazine for teenagers about the use of social networking websites.

1 Think about your audience for this task. Write two or three sentences explaining:

    a) their level of interest in, and attitude to, this topic

    b) why your readers might want or need to know what you have to tell them

    c) what they already know about this topic.

2 Look again at the types of material you ranked in Activity 2. Write down five or more types of material you could include in this task.

ResultsPlus
Controlled assessment tip

List the different sorts of material that you are considering including in your own controlled assessment task. Then put these into rank order, thinking about which are most important for your audience.

Activity 4

Look at the sentences below. Each one is the first sentence of a paragraph taken from one student's response to the task in Activity 3.

1 Which of these sentences would you include in your response to the task? Which would you not include? For each one, write a sentence or two explaining your decision.

    a) | If you're not sure what a social networking site is, or how to use one, let me explain.

    b) | Facebook was started by Mark Zuckerberg, Eduardo Saverin, Dustin Moskovitz and Chris Hughes in 2004.

    c) | Newspaper reports have suggested that social networking sites are dangerously addictive.

    d) | Furthermore, it has been suggested that social networking sites are costing UK businesses millions of pounds every day as workers spend time networking when they should be doing something else.

    e) | It was when I discovered my dad had signed up to the same social networking site as me that I realised it was time to move on.

ResultsPlus
Build better answers

Look at this controlled assessment task:
Write a letter to parents informing them of some of the after-school activities run by your school.

🔲 A Band 3 answer will have a **clear sense of audience** throughout the writing, with the level of formality being largely appropriate for the audience. For parents, this would mean writing formally so that the letter sounds professional.

⚫ A Band 4 answer will sustain this sense of formality throughout and **select the right tone for the audience**, whether this is amusing, serious or confrontational, etc.

🔺 A Band 5 answer will be **sharply focused** on the needs of the audience. It will understand the sorts of question and the reassurance that an audience of parents would need.

4 Writing for your audience: style and tone

This lesson will help you to...

→ achieve the right style and tone for your given audience

You need to choose the **style** of language that is most appropriate for your audience. Your writing will be assessed partly according to how successfully you tailor your style to your audience.

It isn't always easy to get your style right. You have to make a judgement about the level of **formality** or **informality** (the **register**) that works best for the audience. If you make the text too complex and formal your readers will be put off and disengaged; if you make it too 'easy' and chatty your readers will feel patronised and disengaged! The register you choose will influence the overall tone of your writing. Remember that whatever tone you use, you should always write clearly and accurately.

Activity 1

Read the two extracts below from articles written for a school magazine on the subject of healthy eating.

Text A

> A healthy diet is important throughout one's life, but it is essential that one maintains a balanced, healthy and nutritious diet during adolescence, as during this period of challenging academic and personal development, the body is undergoing rapid growth and hormonal change. Young people should avoid over-indulgence in fatty convenience food and ensure their intake includes generous portions of fresh fruit and vegetables.

Text B

> You may be pretty bored with the whole 'you can't eat this, you must eat that' health food fascism that you get force fed daily, but listen up – the well-oiled machine that is your growing body needs some seriously high octane rocket fuel, and fast-food burgers, instant noodles and pizza just ain't gonna cut it. You want to blitz those spots, get yourself some energy, and beat the blues – well, reach for the fruit and veg. Yep, 'five a day' may be corny but it will make you fire away!

1 Say which version you think the editor of the magazine should choose to print, and why.

2 Identify three words or phrases from each version that contribute most to its feeling of formality or informality.

3 Write a third version which sits somewhere between the two in terms of formality.

There are many possible audiences for a piece of writing on healthy eating in schools. It could be your fellow students, younger students, teachers, your head teacher, or parents. You would need to write in a different style for each of these audiences by using a different register and tone. You would also need to consider your use of grammar and choice of vocabulary.

Activity 2

Below are three opening sentences for three texts on the subject of healthy eating. Suggest which one is most suited to each of the following different audiences and give reasons why:

1 Younger students

2 Parents

3 Head teacher

A   On behalf of the students of this school, I am appealing to you to address an aspect of our lives that affects our educational and physical well-being.

B   What you eat is important. It affects not just how you grow, but how well you do at school. It is good to have a choice, but part of growing up is learning to make the right choice.

C   As children of hard-working and concerned parents, we really appreciate (though we may not show it!) the care with which the weekly shop at the supermarket is carried out … plenty of fruit and veg for our 'five-a-day', not too many instant noodles, and easy on those chocs!

It can be easy to forget the effect of pronouns on style and tone. You need to decide whether it is appropriate to use:

- First person singular ('I', 'me') – this is more appropriate for personal letters or blogs than for formal writing.

- First person plural ('we') – this often sounds more professional and authoritative than 'I'. It includes both reader and writer.

- Second person ('you') – this is used most often if you know your audience or if you want to persuade your reader. It is used less in formal texts.

- Third person **active** ('Some people might say …') and **passive** voice ('It is thought that …', 'It is said to be …')

Activity 3

Consider the following tasks.

1 For each one decide why you might make frequent, occasional, or no use at all of the pronouns 'I'/'me', 'we' and 'you', and the third person active or passive voices.

a) A letter to the editor of a newspaper or magazine

b) A persuasive article in the same publication

c) A contribution to an online forum

5 Writing in the right form

This lesson will help you to...

→ understand and use the appropriate genre conventions for your task

As well as defining the purpose and audience of your writing, your task will also specify the form that you have to write in. You may be asked to write for onscreen or paper-based genres such as:

- an article
- a report
- a website
- a review

- a podcast script
- a blog
- a leaflet
- a forum posting

Each of these forms has its own **conventions** – these are the principal 'ingredients' of a particular form of writing. To achieve the highest grades you will need to show that you are familiar with these and to use them effectively in your own writing.

Activity 1

Look at the opening lines below from four different texts responding to a proposal to raise the school leaving age from 16 to 18.

Text A

Does anyone think this is the right thing to do? It's like taking an axe to perform heart surgery. It's a typical, badly thought-out solution as more and more young people are failed by our centralised school system.

Text B

Dear Secretary of State

I am writing to express my opposition to the proposed raising of the school leaving age to 18…

Text C

Children, Schools and Families Secretary Ed Balls today set out the building blocks that will underpin government plans to raise the school leaving age (education participation age) to 17 by 2013 and 18 by 2015.

Text D

Hello and welcome. Do you think it's a good idea to compel all students to stay on in education until their 18th birthday? In today's broadcast we will look at this controversial issue.

1 Identify the form of text that each opening line is taken from.

2 For each opening, identify the genre conventions – the 'clues' that reveal what kind of text each is.

Activity 2

Read the boxes below.

1 Match the form in the left-hand column with the appropriate set of 'ingredients' in the right-hand column.

Form	Ingredients
Article	• Includes a mixture of description, explanation and evaluation • Provides basic information about the product or event • Avoids 'spoilers', i.e. doesn't give too much away
Letter	• Will have a powerful, informative headline • Uses extended sections of detailed text written in continuous paragraphs • Is normally fairly formal in tone • Often draws on statistics and quotations from reliable stated sources
Blog	• Usually includes the address of the author, begins 'Dear …' and concludes with some kind of sign-off • The way the reader is addressed and the way the author signs off vary in formality
Review	• Use of short, clear paragraphs of text • May include extra key facts/extra information in bullet form • Catchy headings • May repeat 'pull quotes' from the body text • Usually includes images with captions
Podcast	• Includes personal observations, combining past-tense narrative with present-tense comment and reflection • May include some less formal, more colloquial forms of language
Leaflet	• May use a combination of different voices, sound effects and music to convey information and ideas • Often includes announcements about what is coming up later

(An arrow is drawn connecting "Letter" to the box beginning "Usually includes the address of the author, begins 'Dear …'")

Activity 3

Look at this extract from an online newspaper article.

1   Identify as many features of the article as you can which are characteristic of this form of writing.

2   Read the article and identify the key points of information contained within it. Write these in bullet point form.

Latest News .co.uk

search [GO]

| Home | News | Sport | Finance | Lifestyle | Comment | Travel | Culture | Technology | Fashion |

| UK | World | UK Politics | Celebrities | Education | World | Science | Topics | News Blog | Videos |

Anger amongst teenagers at government plans to raise school leaving age

Plans to raise the school leaving age to 18 are causing resentment among some teens who believe they will be confined to a classroom studying subjects they are not interested in, new research suggests.

A study by the Youth Commission has found that roughly a third of teenagers (31 per cent) are against new government proposals which would mean students have to stay in education until the age of 18.

Under new legislation, the school leaving age would be raised to 17 by 2013, and 18 by 2015.

While the majority of young people support the new policy (58 per cent), it was revealed that a significant number have concerns about the studying options they will have if they are made to stay on.

It said: "We have found that several of the young people we interviewed have concerns about the lack of choice they perceive will face them if they choose to stay until 18.

"Although this may not be the case in reality, this is the message that has filtered through to them.

"This is causing anger and resentment among those who believe that increasing the school leaving age will mean that they will be forced into the same experiences that led to their initial disengagement with the education system."

One 13-year-old boy told researchers: "I think it's a bad idea. What if I want to leave school or college, get a job and earn some money?"

And a 19-year-old girl said: "Staying in school until you're 18 is good, as long as it is tailored and non-prescriptive, and offers a full range of practical subjects."

If a task asks you to write in a form which involves the spoken word, such as the script for a podcast or a speech, you need to think carefully about how your writing will impact on the ear, as opposed to the eye, of your audience.

Activity 4

1   Write an opening for each of the following texts about the proposal to raise the school leaving age, using the appropriate genre conventions.

   a) **A blog** for young people recording your own personal observations and reflections on the issue.

   b) **A contribution to an online forum** for adults arguing the case either in favour of or against the proposal.

   c) **A podcast** for an educational website considering the pros and cons of the proposal.

   d) **A newspaper article** discussing various aspects of the issue in depth.

2   Write the whole text in response to **one** of these tasks.

Here is an example of a controlled assessment task you could be expected to answer.

In your response to this task you would be expected to write using the conventions, or features, of a magazine article.

> Write an article for your school magazine in which you explain why school is important to you.
>
> (20 marks)

Activity 5

Write the opening two paragraphs of the article explaining why school is important to you.

You should focus on using the right conventions, or features, of an article.

You should spend 15 minutes on this task.

ResultsPlus
Self assessment

Before you complete this self-assessment activity, you might like to read some sample answers to this task on the following pages (72 – 73).

1 **Check your answer to Activity 5:**
   - Did you open your article with a powerful headline and succinct opening paragraph?
   - Did you include features such as expert opinion and facts to give the feel of an article?
   - Did you get the right balance between entertaining and informing?
   - Did you use a variety of sentences that are common in articles?

2 **Now decide which Band your answer to Activity 5 should fall into by applying the mark scheme opposite. You will need to be careful and precise in your marking.**

Band 3
- ideas are appropriate to an article and effectively developed
- vocabulary is well-chosen
- evidence of crafting when constructing sentences

Band 4
- ideas are presented effectively as an article and sustained throughout
- vocabulary is aptly chosen
- well-controlled variety of sentences

Band 5
- consistent fulfilment of task
- extensive vocabulary
- varied and sophisticated control of sentences

Maximise your marks

Write the opening two paragraphs of the article explaining why school is important to you. You should focus on using the right conventions, or features, of an article.

Here are three student answers to the article task on page 71. Read the answers together with the examiner comments around and after the answers. Then complete the activity at the bottom of page 73.

Student 1 – Extract typical of a grade (B) answer

An effective opening that grabs the reader immediately. This idea is carried on throughout the article. To engage the reader this way is important when writing a newspaper article.

> Jail or Gateway?
> Our school: a tall, red brick building that looms over the concrete yard. Frames criss-cross the towering windows and padlocks hang from doors and gates... It's possible that if they want us to stop viewing school as a prison that they should stop building them to look like some hideous torture chamber! In all seriousness – is this place just a jail for children or is it our gateway to the future we need?
> Endless generations of kids have sat staring out of windows wishing for the bell to ring. The desire for freedom, to get out of the uniform, to just... just... sit for hours in front of the television is too much for them. For these kids school has all the features of prison.

Some clever vocabulary makes the writer of the article sound like they are an authority.

Examiner summary

This part of the answer is typical of a grade B performance. Opening with the description of the school as a jail is really effective. This is then sustained throughout. The choice of vocabulary makes the article sound like it has authority and the use of exclamations and ellipses shows that the student has control over a variety of sentences.

Student 2 – Extract typical of a grade (A) answer

A clever, emotive headline that is fitting for an article and shows the student is focused on the task.

> I feared I would live alone on the streets.
> At 15, when things were spiralling out of control at home, I forgot why I was at school. I was angry and was punishing the world: by failing my exams. That would show them!
> Teachers, well, they were an annoyance. Asking how I was, still insisting I complete the work, always there... buzzing, buzzing around my head, snipping at me like a mosquito. They didn't care about me. All those friends everywhere pretending that they cared for me – they were just interested in the intrigue – the hum of social workers and possible court cases. I was alone then and thought I would be alone now.

Effective repetition that turns into an extended metaphor.

Examiner summary

This part of the answer is typical of a grade A performance. It is an idea that uses emotion to grab the audience and draw them into the article. The short paragraphs are characteristic of an article and show a secure realisation of the task. The language is original at times but the lack of development and simplistic vocabulary choices prevent this from being marked higher.

Strong language choices show the student has an extensive vocabulary.

Varied sentence form communicates the irony in the student's tone of voice.

Gimme the money!

"People who leave university with a degree will earn £200,000 more in their lifetime than those who do not" — a fact flourished by the government in a drive to drag us all back into education. "Children who are home schooled struggle to build fulfilling relationships in later life"; so says the Child and Welfare Committee. Making money, building a family — what else is there to life? Of course school is important!

Yet, you feel that these civil servants have missed the point. Have they been in a school for 6 hours each day and witnessed the struggle of students piling through the corridors? It is hard to imagine the future money and the potential partner. You are more worried about whether going to the toilet will result in a bruise between your shoulders.

Use of statistics and expert quotations shows the student is very aware of the form and audience of the writing.

Examiner summary

This part of the answer is typical of a grade A* performance. There is an authoritative tone to the article that is maintained through the paragraphs. The use of vocabulary helps the idea seem exciting to the reader as words like 'flourish' and 'drag' have appropriate connotations.

ResultsPlus
Build better answers

**Move from a Grade to Grade **

In this part of the task you need to add power to your response to compel your audience to continue reading. Student 1 has an interesting idea but it is a fairly common metaphor and is not as interesting as the personal testimony of Student 2.

**Aim for a Grade **

In this part of the task you need to develop ideas and show consistency. Student 2's response is clever but the paragraphs are short and the points feel brief. The choice to use paragraphs may have been made on purpose to match the conventions of tabloid newspapers but the writing and ideas need to be developed further.

Putting it into practice

1. Write the opening two paragraphs of a blog about school.

2. Compare the choices you made for the article and the choices you made for the blog.

6 Generating ideas

In the world of writing, journalism and publishing, writers often work to a brief provided by their editors which defines the nature of the text they are commissioned to produce. It is likely to specify the **purpose**, **audience** and **form** of the writing. You should think of your controlled assessment task as a similar exercise, so you need to examine your task carefully.

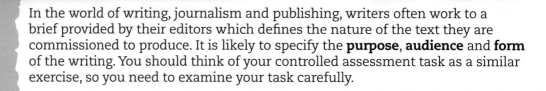

Activity 1

Look at this example of a controlled assessment task:

> Write an article for a magazine in which you persuade readers about an environmental issue from a specific point of view.

1 Identify the key elements of purpose, audience and form.

Whatever the subject of your writing task, you will need to include a mixture of information and ideas (and possibly your own informed opinions, too). These ideas will come from three sources:

- ideas, information and opinions you already have (which may come from the texts you have studied for the reading task)
- ideas you can develop, imagine or invent
- information you need to research.

In order to record the initial ideas, information and opinions you already have about this subject you could use a simple brainstorming technique, a spider diagram or a basic list.

Activity 2

1 Now generate and record the ideas you would include in your response to the task from Activity 1. You might want to use a spider diagram or a list.

Another helpful strategy for generating ideas is to draft a list of questions. Asking yourself the right kinds of question can help you develop your ideas on a topic by prompting you to formulate detailed answers. This will also tell you how much research you might still need to do.

For example, if you were preparing to write a contribution to an online forum on the subject of violent computer games, you could ask yourself:

- What effect might violence in computer games have on people who play them? Why?
- What restrictions (if any) should there be on the kinds of violence shown in these games? Why?
- What age limits (if any) should be imposed on the sale of these games? Why?

Activity ③

1 Draft five questions that you could ask yourself in order to generate ideas in response to the question from Activity 1.

2 Answer the questions as fully as you can. Make a note of any areas that would need further research.

There will still be things you need to find out for yourself before you can write with conviction and authority about your topic. You can find out more about your chosen topic in several ways.

Activity ④

1 Copy and complete the table below, identifying the advantages and disadvantages of some common research techniques. Some spaces have been filled in for you.

Source/method	Advantages	Disadvantages
Internet searches		Not always reliable – websites might be biased; might not be written by experts; might be out of date
Paper-based research – books, newspapers, magazines		
Talking to your friends and teachers about what they know and think	Easy and quick. Most people will have some ideas and views on the topic	
Finding things out first hand – talking to experts, visiting places, etc.		Could be time-consuming and impractical; might not be possible to visit a wind-farm or talk to an expert scientist or engineer!
Designing and conducting a questionnaire or survey, e.g. on people's attitudes, habits, opinions, etc.	Will produce some useful 'real' findings which you can refer to in your piece of writing	

ResultsPlus
Controlled assessment tip

When writing your final response to your controlled assessment task, you must be careful to avoid **plagiarism**. This is using other people's words and pretending that they are your own. To ensure you submit your own original work, you should:

- keep brief the notes you are going to take into your controlled assessment.

- use quotation marks for any passages of text which you have taken from someone else's work and state as clearly as possible where these are from.

7 Planning your writing

This lesson will help you to...

→ **plan your writing**
→ **create an effective structure**

As you prepare for your controlled assessment task you need to make the most of the opportunity to think carefully in advance about what you are going to write and the structure of the text you will produce. You will be able to consult the notes you have made in preparation for the task, which should include some plans for the text you are going to write.

Once you have generated all the ideas you wish to include and have done your research for your controlled assessment task, you will need to work out how you are going to order them within your writing in a logical way. This planning process is sometimes called **sequencing**.

Below is an example of one student's ideas for inclusion in a controlled assessment task on the topic of animal welfare.

Proper ways of looking after pets

Wrong reasons for buying a pet (related to RSPCA)

Number of animals on UK farms to meet demand

How suitable living conditions are ensured

Pets

Stray and lost pets

Animals in farming

Guidelines that exist for humane slaughter

Work of the organisation and why it's important

Amount of meat consumed in the UK per year

RSPCA

Animal welfare

Write an article for a teenage magazine to raise awareness of the issue of animal welfare.

Worst cases of abuse encountered and success stories

Animals used in business (link to animal testing)

Cases of protests in the past (e.g. Huntingdon Life Sciences)

Animals and the law

Animal testing

Illegal treatment of animals and punishments

Why animals are used for testing

Government legislation to protect animals – is it sufficient?

In what cases it is allowed (linked to Animals and the law)

Possible cruelty and how it should be prevented

Action

Volunteer

Be aware and report instances of cruelty

Support the RSPCA

Activity 1

Here are some ideas for the content of the article on animal welfare, summarised in no particular order.

1 Decide on the best sequence for these ideas in the article.

- Looking after pets and problems with abandoned/neglected dogs and cats
- Farm welfare issues, e.g. factory farming of hens
- The role of the RSPCA and its animal rescue centres
- Animals used in scientific research, e.g. for testing new drugs
- An overview of the whole question of the treatment of animals by humans
- What the law says about animal cruelty

When you come to decide on a final structure for your piece of writing, you will need to think about the purpose, audience and form of your writing, and there are several possible models for structure that you can follow.

Type of structure	Chronological sequence	Balanced view	Argument	Information
Sequence of ideas in structure	What happened first ↓ Events that followed ↓ Final event	Overview of topic ↓ Points for ↓ Points against ↓ Conclusion	Overview of topic and introduce conclusion ↓ Give reasons for conclusion and evidence in support of this (and perhaps reasons for dismissing the counter-arguments) ↓ Restate conclusion	Summary of key points/issues ↓ Expansion of key points ↓ Restate key points with summary
Advantage of each type of structure	Useful for tasks which involve an aspect of **narrative**, or storytelling	Useful for **discussions** of controversial topics where you are asked to review different points of view	Useful where you are asked to make a case or an **argument** in favour of a particular point of view	Useful for **articles** where you try to grab the attention of readers in the opening paragraph

Activity 2

1 Choose which structure you would use for the article on animal welfare. Why did you choose this structure? What information will come first and what will come at the end?

2 Now work out how you will sequence and structure the ideas you have for your response to the task in Activity 1 on page 74. Prepare to give a short presentation of your plans either to your teacher or to a group of fellow students in which you explain the reasons behind your planning.

8 Structure

This lesson will help you to...

→ write an effective opening
→ write well-constructed paragraphs

The opening few sentences of your text are vital. An effective opening can hook your readers into the rest of your piece. What makes an opening effective depends on the audience, purpose and form of your writing, but there are some techniques that you can use.

Activity 1

Below are several openings, all of which have been written for a podcast aimed at young listeners to introduce them to the work of the street graffiti artist Banksy.

Technique	Example
Ask the question(s) which the text will go on to answer. Try creating a group of three.	The work of Banksy raises many questions. Is it art, or merely vandalism? Should he be prosecuted or given a knighthood? And perhaps above all – who is he, anyway?
Address the audience directly using the second person. Get them to place themselves in the situation.	Picture the scene. You are walking down a city street and you see a hooded figure crouched in front of a wall, spray can in hand. What is your reaction?
Use **shock tactics** to grab the attention of your audience.	One image shows a uniformed guardsman apparently being patted down by a young girl; in another mural two policemen engage in an affectionate embrace; in a third, a small boy with a fishing rod appears to have caught a hypodermic syringe. Art? Or mindless vandalism?
Use a **human interest** 'angle' to introduce a topic.	The artist known as 'Banksy' remains a mystery – he seems to have originated from the Bristol area, and may be in his 30s or 40s. Some images claiming to show him at work reveal a scruffy, hooded, bespectacled figure.
Give a brief summary of the **main facts** of your piece: •What has happened? •Where did it happen? •Who was involved and affected? •When did it all happen?	For years the identity of graffiti artist 'Banksy' has remained mysterious, but a British newspaper has claimed today that 'Banksy' is in fact a 34-year-old called Robin Gunningham.
Build up an element of suspense or mystery – using pronouns (like 'he') before revealing who, or what, your piece is actually about.	He is one of the best-known names in modern art; his work appears mysteriously overnight; he receives no payment – and despite the recent release of a film about his work, his identity remains shrouded in mystery. So who, exactly, is Banksy?

1 Note down the possible advantages and disadvantages of each of the approaches for this podcast. Decide on a rank order for them in terms of their effectiveness.

2 Decide which of the techniques might be appropriate for a newspaper review of a film you have watched recently. Remember to think about the audience, purpose and form. Try writing a couple of drafts for the opening of the article, using two of these techniques.

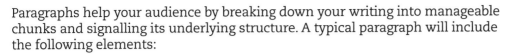

Paragraphs help your audience by breaking down your writing into manageable chunks and signalling its underlying structure. A typical paragraph will include the following elements:

- **Topic sentence:** the first sentence of a paragraph will often be a broad statement of the topic that the paragraph will explore.

- **Development:** most of the remainder of the paragraph will develop this topic in detail, including relevant facts, examples and/or quotations.

- **Closure:** a paragraph will sometimes end with some kind of mini conclusion.

Remember that paragraphs do not always have this structure, however, and good writers will vary the structure of paragraphs for both variety and effect.

Activity 2

Look at the five sentences below. They are from a paragraph of an online article about an exhibition of Banksy's work in his home town of Bristol, but they have been jumbled up.

A Even Bristol City Council chiefs were kept in the dark until the day before it opened.

B It's entitled 'Banksy vs Bristol Museum' and will feature more than 100 pieces, 70 of them new works.

C It's official, Banksy's Summer Show will take place at the Bristol Museum (we knew that) and will run from 13 June to 31 August 2009.

D Museum director Kate Brindley was relieved to finally be able to talk about the exhibition after months of secrecy.

E The show, which only a handful of Museum officials knew about, has taken months to plan.

1 **Arrange the sentences in the right order. Start by identifying the topic sentence.**

As well as the structure of your individual paragraphs, you will need to think about the cohesion of your text as a whole. You can use several devices to help with this:

- **Titles, headings and subheadings** – these act as signposts through the text.

- **Connecting words and phrases** – these can show that you are adding something (e.g. 'in addition', 'moreover'), that you are introducing a contrast (e.g. 'however', 'on the other hand') or that you are leading to a conclusion (e.g. 'because', 'as a result').

- **References forwards and backwards** – these remind your audience what is to come or what they have already read (e.g. 'as we will see', 'as already stated').

You can read more about cohesive devices on pages 108–109.

Activity 3

Look again at the paragraph about Banksy's Bristol show which you reassembled in Activity 2.

1 Identify the features of the text that enabled you to reassemble it.

2 Write the opening part of a script for a podcast aimed at young people aged 11–14 in which you inform them about an environmental issue. Think about the way in which you structure your writing using cohesive devices.

ResultsPlus
Build better answers

Look at this controlled assessment task:

Write a review for a film magazine which comments on a recent film you have seen.

When your writing as a whole is assessed the following criteria will be used to decide which Band it should fall into:

■ A Band 3 answer will have **a clear text structure** that will have an **opening, development and closure**.

● A Band 4 answer will have a **secure** structure. It will have a **well-judged** order to the paragraphs.

▲ A Band 5 answer will be **convincing**, with **sophisticated control of text structure**. The reader will be convinced that you knew what conclusion you were going to draw when you began writing.

9 Crafting vocabulary

This lesson will help you to...

→ select vocabulary appropriate to the formality required by your audience and purpose

→ convey meanings precisely and use vocabulary imaginatively

It is possible to express very similar ideas using a number of different levels of formality or **register**, ranging from the very formal to the highly **colloquial** (or even slang) along with different degrees of **technical** language. Your choice of register will depend on your audience and purpose and the form you are writing in.

Activity 1

Look at this example of a controlled assessment task:

> Write an article for an online magazine on the subject of illegal music downloads.

1 Place these five sentences from drafts of the article in order of register, ranging from 1 (most formal) to 5 (highly colloquial). Make a note of the reasons for your choices, paying particular attention to vocabulary.

A
> In the last few years loads of websites have sprung up making it easy to download music for free, with the result that the people involved in making music receive less money.

B
> It's a doddle to download any amount of music stuff nowadays 'innit, but the suits are all whingeing about all the dough they're missing out on.

C
> The rapid development of web-based file-sharing technology has led to an epidemic of illegal downloading which threatens the future viability of the music business as we know it.

D
> Internet and digital recording technologies have greatly facilitated intellectual property piracy in the field of musical production with inevitably severe financial consequences for stakeholders in the industry.

E
> It's got really easy to get your music for free via the internet but this means that the musos who create the stuff are getting less cash.

2 Write the opening and the first three paragraphs of the article for the online magazine. Think about what register is appropriate for the audience and purpose of your writing: how formal, informal, or colloquial should your vocabulary be?

Choosing the right words is about much more than just creating the right register. The English language offers a rich variety of words to express a single idea, which may be very close in their surface meaning (these are called **synonyms**), but there will be subtle differences between the associations and what they imply – their **connotations**.

Activity ②   Look at this sentence:

Downloading music illegally is a kind of stealing.

If you look up the word 'steal' in a thesaurus you might be given these synonyms:

> **Steal**: abduct, appropriate, blackmail, burglarise, carry off, cheat, cozen, defraud, despoil, divert, embezzle, heist, hold for ransom, hold up, housebreak, keep, kidnap, lift*, loot, make off with, misappropriate, peculate, pilfer, pillage, pinch*, pirate, plagiarise, plunder, poach, purloin, ransack, remove, rifle, rip off, run off with, sack, shoplift, snitch, spirit away, stick up, strip, swindle, swipe, take, take possession of, thieve, walk off with, withdraw
>
> * = informal/non-formal usage   Text used courtesy of www.thesaurus.com

1   Organise these synonyms into groups of words that have something in common, e.g. words that imply some element of violence such as 'pillage' and 'despoil', or words that imply the thing being stolen is cheap or trivial. Use a dictionary if you don't know the meaning of some of these words.

2   Select just two or three of these words that it might be appropriate to use in the article on illegal downloading from Activity 1. Write three further paragraphs of the article you began in Activity 1, thinking about the connotations of the words that you use.

Results Plus
Controlled assessment tip

Using a thesaurus can be helpful as you prepare for your controlled assessment. **Don't** attempt to use words you have never met before, but **do** use it to help you find just the right word for the meaning you are trying to express. But … be wary! Words will have slightly different nuances of meaning and using them inappropriately can reveal weakness in your control of language.

The most effective writing of all often surprises its audience with its flair and originality and there are some 'dos and don'ts' you can apply to your own writing as you strive to achieve this:

Do:	Don't:
• think twice about your choice of vocabulary • create 'colour' by thinking of unusual comparisons, metaphors and images • take some 'risks' by trying an unpredictable approach.	• go for the first words that come into your head (e.g. 'nice') – they're probably the same **clichés** that occur to everyone else! • **exaggerate** or **overstate** (e.g. 'huge' is an overused word!) unless you are doing it for effect, e.g. humour • try to be too clever: sometimes simplicity and clarity can go a long way.

10 Crafting sentences

This lesson will help you to...

→ use a variety of sentence structures to achieve a range of effects

As you write, you need to show you can use a range of sentence structures effectively. This means using differing **kinds** of sentence (statements, questions, commands) at different points in your text and varying the length of sentences to achieve a particular effect. You should also consider how complex you will make your sentences and how to order your words within sentences.

There are four types of sentence:

- **statements** – these sentences convey information or ideas (like this one)
- **interrogatives** – these sentences ask questions (is that clear?)
- **imperatives** – these sentences give direct commands (take note)
- **exclamations** – these sentences do what they say (what an easy concept!)

You are likely to make more use of some than of others, depending on the kind of text you are planning to write – if you are sharing information, you'll be using mainly statements. Imperatives will be useful if you are giving advice or instructions. All of these sentences can be different lengths. Long, complex sentences are sometimes needed to develop complex ideas but contrasting these with short sentences can create a powerful impact.

Activity Look at this example of a controlled assessment task:

> Write a contribution to an online forum on the subject of gang-related crime and its causes.

Consider these two versions of contributions to the online forum. They use the same words and the same ideas but different sentence lengths.

1 Decide which version you think would be more effective and explain why.

Text A

news | sport | business | entertainment | money
yourviewsforum

Some people argue that stiffer punishments such as automatic prison sentences and more tightly enforced stop-and-search laws would clamp down on knife-carrying and thus reduce violent crime on our streets among young people. Unfortunately, as this fails to take into account the underlying reasons that young people choose to carry knives in the first place, complex as these are, it is far too simplistic a solution. We also need to address the problems of educational underachievement, lack of opportunities, social deprivation and economic hardship that drive these youngsters into the world of gangs and knife crime in the first place.

Text B

opinions.com

Some people argue that stiffer punishments are the answer. Impose automatic prison sentences. Enforce the stop-and-search laws. Clamp down on knife-carrying. This would reduce violent crime on our streets among young people. Unfortunately, this fails to take into account the underlying reasons that young people choose to carry knives in the first place. These are complex. The solution is far too simplistic. We also need to address the problems of educational underachievement. We need to address the lack of opportunities. We need to address the social deprivation and economic hardship that drive these youngsters into the world of gangs and knife crime in the first place.

Sometimes you can create subtly different effects depending on the word order (or **syntax**) of a sentence. Being able to do this effectively will help you to achieve the highest grades.

Activity ➋

Imagine you are drafting your own contribution to the forum on the same topic as the previous activity.

1   Consider the sentences below which are alternative syntactical choices. In each case select the version you think would be most effective, and give your reasons.

> a) A Knife crime is one of the biggest problems facing urban Britain today.
>
> B It's one of the biggest problems facing Britain today – knife crime.

> b) A As a result of some high-profile incidents, people have gradually come to realise that something needs to be done
>
> B Gradually, and after some high-profile incidents, people have come to realise that something needs to be done.

> c) A We need to address the underlying causes of the problem.
>
> B The underlying causes of the problem need to be addressed.

Activity ➌

1   Write your own paragraph in response to the task in Activity 1, and practise varying the way you construct the sentences in your own writing.

ResultsPlus
Watch out!

Questions are an effective device for creating tone in writing. However, the key to success is variety. Use powerful language devices such as rhetorical questions sparingly and they will retain their impact on the reader.

ResultsPlus
Self assessment

Check your answer – have you:

- ensured you use clear and accurate sentence structure?

- thought about how your sentences can be structured to convey exactly the right expressive tone and meaning?

- included a variety of sentence lengths and structures for effect?

You can also look at pages 146–147 for further information on crafting sentences.

11 Crafting punctuation

This lesson will help you to...

→ use the full range of punctuation effectively

Using punctuation effectively is more than just remembering where to put your full stops. Getting the basics right is obviously important, but skilful writers can also manipulate punctuation subtly to create precise meanings and effects.

In general, punctuation has two distinct functions:

• to clarify **meaning** by flagging up the structure of phrases and sentences

• to convey **tone**, equivalent to the way we use our voices in spoken language.

If you are aiming for the higher grades in your controlled assessment, the mark scheme demands that you use punctuation accurately and with maximum effect. You need to be confident about using full stops, question marks, exclamation marks, capital letters, speech marks, apostrophes and commas.

Activity 1

Below is a student's draft of part of a webpage aimed at youngsters about the dangers of over-exposure to the sun and tanning machines.

1 Rewrite it, making any corrections and amendments to the punctuation that you think are required.

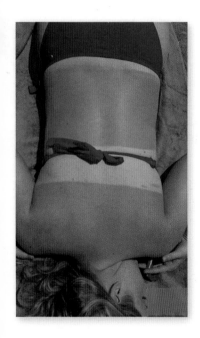

> Many of us like a tan and spend a lot of time and money getting one we like to holiday in the sun we like to go to hot places and spend hours basking in the strong sunshine everywhere from the Costa Brava to the Caribbean. Or we may have to settle for a few hours lying on a sunbed in the local tanning salon. We think it makes us look attractive and feel healthy but how much do we know or care about the harm we may be doing. We ll be fine if we slap on a bit of suncream and besides its only older people that get skin cancer isnt it? As for looking like a wrinkly old rhino by the time youre 40 well it won't matter by then will it.
>
> If this sounds like you, its time to open your eyes. Is there such a thing as a healthy tan. Or can it be cool to be pale.

One of the most frequent punctuation errors is the use of the comma instead of a different form of punctuation. Many students develop this bad habit, as in this example:

Sunbathing isn't good for your skin, a sun tan is in fact a sign of skin damage.

Instead of a comma, a connective like 'and', a dash or a semi-colon would be appropriate. Dashes can also be used to introduce ideas and information instead of brackets, or to inject a touch of drama.

Activity 2

Look at the two versions below of an online article about tanning. One of them uses dashes.

1 Decide which version you think is more effective and explain why.

Text A

Career & Money | Health | Parenting | Personal Growth | Relationships | Religion

Tanning - Dangers of Too Much Sun

Sunburns and blistering are the most obvious – and painful – results of short-term sun damage. The long-term damage, such as wrinkling, can be disfiguring and, in the case of skin cancer, possibly life-threatening.

Barbara Gilchrest, M.D. – chairman of the department of dermatology, Boston University School of Medicine – explains that you can think of the skin damage as happening along parallel tracks that intertwine. Freckling and wrinkling are at one end of the tracks, and skin cancer looms at the other end.

The cosmetic changes – wrinkling, coarseness, and irregular pigmentation – occur on one track. The more sinister changes, such as actinic keratosis – scaly, rough, and red, tan, brownish, or greyish spots on the skin that can lead to cancerous tumours — occur on the other.

Text B

Career & Money | Health | Parenting | Personal Growth | Relationships | Religion

Tanning - Dangers of Too Much Sun

Sunburns and blistering are the most obvious and painful results of short-term sun damage. The long-term damage, such as wrinkling, can be disfiguring and, in the case of skin cancer, possibly life-threatening.

Barbara Gilchrest, M.D., chairman of the department of dermatology, Boston University School of Medicine, explains that you can think of the skin damage as happening along parallel tracks that intertwine. Freckling and wrinkling are at one end of the tracks, and skin cancer looms at the other end.

The cosmetic changes (wrinkling, coarseness, and irregular pigmentation) occur on one track. The more sinister changes, such as actinic keratosis (scaly, rough, and red, tan, brownish, or greyish spots on the skin that can lead to cancerous tumours) occur on the other.

Question marks, exclamations and ellipses can be used to suggest aspects of tone as you write. They can help your audience to 'hear' your voice and the attitude you wish to convey. These devices can suggest various degrees of enthusiasm, irony, surprise and disbelief.

ResultsPlus
Controlled assessment tip

Think of punctuation like the baton of a conductor of an orchestra. Punctuation controls the pace, emphasis and nuance of the text. Listen to the words in your mind and think: how can I use punctuation to direct my reader to read it in that way?

Activity 3

Read the text below. It is part of a student's draft of an article for a school magazine, describing a memorable holiday.

1 Suggest where the following punctuation features could improve the effect of the writing:

a) use of an ellipsis to build up a feeling of suspense or expectation

b) use of a pair of dashes to emphasise the delay to the plane

c) replacement of a comma with a dash to create a sense of irony

d) replacement of excessive exclamation marks throughout the text – suggest appropriate alternatives.

It is said that part of the pleasure of any holiday is the anticipation, our trip to Spain in 2008 was no exception! We felt the usual excitement as we rushed around packing our bags before setting off for the airport. Little did we know as we queued at the busy check-in desk what lay ahead.

The flight to Spain was eventually quite uneventful, though after waiting for nearly three hours in a stuffy departure lounge we were starting to wonder if we would ever reach our destination! In fact our troubles all lay ahead of us! After collecting our bags we were transferred by coach to our 'luxurious beach apartment overlooking the azure Mediterranean sea', or so it said in the brochure. When we finally saw it we couldn't believe our eyes!

Activity 4

1 Write three paragraphs of a magazine article in which you review a recent holiday you have been on. Try to use as wide a variety of punctuation as possible to communicate accurately and convey tone.

Here is an example of a controlled assessment task you could be expected to answer. In your response to this task you will be expected to use punctuation effectively.

> Write the first entry of a blog to inform teenagers about a trip that you are taking.
>
> (20 marks)

Results Plus

Watch out!

Don't be tempted to use too many questions or exclamation marks – they can become tiresome for the reader. Only ever use one exclamation mark or question mark at a time!

Activity 5

Write the opening paragraph of the blog for teenagers. Focus on the variety and effectiveness of the punctuation that you use.

You should spend 15 minutes on this task.

Results Plus

Self assessment

Before you complete this self-assessment activity, you might like to read some sample answers to this task on the following pages (88 –89).

1 **Check your answer to Activity 5:**
   - Did you use a variety of punctuation marks, including question marks, exclamation marks and semi-colons?
   - Did you consider how the punctuation you use could help you to shape the meaning of your work?
   - Did you consider the tone of voice and pace you wanted to create and select the most effective punctuation to achieve this?

2 **Now decide which Band your answer to Activity 5 should fall into by applying the mark scheme opposite. You will need to be careful and precise in your marking.**

■ **Band 3**
   - uses punctuation that has an impact on the reader and makes important ideas stand out
   - includes clear and accurate sentences, with control over the way the reader reads the text

● **Band 4**
   - uses punctuation precisely to create the effects intended
   - includes well-structured sentences, with effective control over the way the reader reads the text

▲ **Band 5**
   - uses punctuation in a sophisticated way that helps to ensure effective emphasis of ideas
   - includes convincingly structured sentences, with sophisticated control over the way the reader reads the text

Write the opening paragraph of the blog for teenagers. Focus on the variety and effectiveness of the punctuation that you use.

Here are three student answers to the blog task on page 87. Read the answers together with the examiner comments around and after the answers. Then complete the activity at the bottom of page 89.

Student 1 – Extract typical of a grade **B** answer

Some variety of punctuation, which supports the intended effect of greeting the audience enthusiastically.

> Hello guys! I just thought I'd inform you of a trip that I have planned abroad. I have many reasons for going on my trip with one example would be the landscape. Scientist George McCann said, "When we experimented on the soil in Italy we found it was the most delicate soft soil we have ever seen. This is due to the wonderful care that the farmers put into the farms. This makes the landscape of Italy truly wonderful!" In my trip I hope to understand this perfect landscape and its historical traditions.

Sentences are accurately structured.

Examiner summary

This part of the answer is typical of grade a B performance. The use of punctuation is precise, with the inclusion of commas and apostrophes, and the sentences are well structured. The use of the exclamation marks is intended to give the effect of excitement. To improve the answer further the student could use punctuation to make the writing seem a little less formal – for example, including dashes and ellipses to show how we pause and connect ideas when speaking. This would give the impression that they were writing a blog.

Student 2 – Extract typical of a grade **A** answer

Clever compound using hyphens – good for creating an informal tone to writing. This shows a high level of punctuation use.

> I have actually just wiggled my fingers and done the finger-cracking-to-prepare-for-genius-typing thing! I am now officially a travel writer. Ok, Ok, so I have to travel first and I am still in my bedroom in Swindon but you know... preparation is everything!
>
> Here are my thoughts so far: catch a bus to the train station; travel to London and catch Eurostar... and that's it. Not the most developed plan in the world, I know. Needs a bit of work. I do have dreams – I want to go to Italy – to see the Colosseum and eat ice cream. I really want to climb the Eiffel Tower and have a French man say words of love to me. And, I want to see if Belgium really is so flat that all you do is pass through. Bruges looked fun in that film!

Use of the ellipses and the exclamation mark show excellent variety of punctuation and show the beginnings of a convincing structure to sentences.

Examiner summary

This part of the answer is typical of a grade A performance. There is good control of expression and the use of the hyphen to compound the list of words is an effective tool for adding excitement to a piece of informal writing. There is also a lot more skill shown in the punctuation, though this could have been used more effectively to emphasise the tricolon in the second paragraph.

I'm on the boat... No time or signal to chat to people (sorry), so I thought I'd write on this blog you lot set up for me so you can make sure that I'm not dead or anything! (Did you know they had internet cafes on ferries now? Weird! Where do the cables go?)

It'll disturb you to know that I actually had no clue where I was heading... Thought I'd plan on the run and add some excitement to the adventure. Stupid, I hear you cry; genius, I think! I've spent the thirty odd hours so far plotting my route like some ancient explorer. A map and a compass (and the world wide web) were my only tools.

The use of parentheses helps to add humour to the writing, giving the snippet inside the brackets a tone of irony.

This use of punctuation is impressive. It is used to create antithesis and control the pace and tone with which this is read.

Examiner summary

This part of the answer is typical of a grade A* performance. The writer has used punctuation, employing ellipses and brackets, to control the tone of voice and to help build humour. The use of antithesis is particularly effective as the student orchestrates the tone of the piece, ensuring the most effective pace and emphasis of words.

ResultsPlus
Build better answers

Move from a Grade Ⓑ to Grade Ⓐ

In this part of the answer you need to employ punctuation to impact on the tone of the writing. Student 1 uses punctuation accurately and there is a good variety of punctuation. However, it was not employed to impact on the pace or tone of the writing, and instead just makes the paragraph grammatically correct. Student 2 begins to understand the control that punctuation gives you over the impact on the reader with the use of compound and ellipsis to give a humorous tone.

Aim for a Grade Ⓐ*

In this part of the answer you need to use punctuation to create subtleties of meaning. Both Student 2 and Student 3 have successfully created an informal and jokey tone to their writing. Student 3, however, uses antithesis and irony with parentheses which could elevate the student to the next grade up.

Putting it into practice

1 **Revisit the opening paragraph for your blog. Experiment with punctuation to create different effects. You might want to try:**

a) **sounding dramatic**

b) **sounding homesick**

Controlled assessment practice

Examiner's tip

Your controlled assessment will be based on a theme. Your writing task will be on the same theme as the texts you have studied for the reading part of this unit.

Examiner's tip

Deciding on the answers to these elements will help you plan your writing.

Examiner's tip

Remember to check over your writing before submitting it. Accuracy is important but do not compromise the ambition of your vocabulary or sentence construction.

Guidance for students: Writing Task

What do I have to do?
You will complete one writing task on the theme of the environment. You must complete this task on your own.

How much time do I have?
Following preparation, you will have up to two hours to complete the task.

How do I prepare for the task?
- Select one task.
- You will be provided with guidance about writing, which may include:
  - the content — real or imagined
  - the audience and purpose
  - the form and structural features of writing
  - the 'voice' you may want to use
  - appropriate language techniques.
- You should then prepare by making notes and planning your response to the task.

What must the response to the task show?
Your response must show that you can:
- make choices in writing that are appropriate to audience and purpose
- spell, punctuate and use grammatical structures that are accurate and appropriate for purpose and effect.

How should I present the response?
A written response of up to 1000 words.

The Writing Task for the student

Complete one task from those below.

EITHER

Write an article for a magazine in which you persuade readers about an environmental issue from a specific point of view.   (20)

OR

Write the script for a podcast for a website for young people aged 11 – 14, where you inform them about an environmental issue.   (20)

Examiner's tip

Pick one task here. Remember to make your response appropriate for the given audience, purpose and form, and use original ideas as far as possible to help you gain the highest grades.

Unit 2 The Writer's Craft
The Writer's Voice

Whether you are taking GCSE English or GCSE English Language, this unit will help you to prepare for the writing task in your examination (Section B in English Language and Section C in English). This task will ask you to write a response to a situation, issue or problem and you'll need to be able to use evidence to support the views and opinions you write about.

This section of the book will help you to build on the writing skills you developed in Unit 1, giving you plenty of strategies for writing effectively under time constraints in an examination. The following lessons explore different ways that you can approach the writing task. The activities you'll complete in this unit are all focused on helping you to achieve the best grade you can in this section of the examination.

Your assessment

Unit 2 is an examination unit. The first part of your examination will focus on the set texts you have studied in class, and the final section will be a writing task which is the focus of this unit of the book. You will have to answer one question from a choice of **two**.

Your response to the writing section must show that you can:

✔ reflect on ideas, issues, experiences and events, rather than writing a narrative or description

✔ write in a form, such as a newspaper article, formal report or magazine review, targeting a specified audience

✔ reflect and comment on contemporary issues, situations or problems that are relevant to you, such as lifestyle, school or college life, local issues or national issues that affect young people.

Assessment Objectives

Your response to this section of the examination will be marked using these Assessment Objectives:

✔ Write clearly, effectively and imaginatively, using and adapting forms and selecting vocabulary appropriate to the task and purpose in ways that engage the reader.

✔ Organise information and ideas into structured and sequenced sentences, paragraphs and whole texts, using a variety of linguistic and structural features to support cohesion and overall coherence.

✔ Use a range of sentence structures for clarity, purpose and effect, with accurate punctuation and spelling.

This student book unit will help you to understand what these require you to do so that you can write a successful response in the examination.

1 Purpose

→ **make choices according to the purpose of the writing task**

In your writing task for the Unit 2 examination, you will need to plan and write a piece of writing within roughly one hour. As for your writing in Unit 1, your response will need to fit the audience, purpose and form specified in the task you are set. The task you are given in the examination will give you a specific purpose for your writing and to achieve the highest grade, you must show that your text will fulfil that purpose. The purpose of your writing will influence both the **content** and **style** of what you choose to write.

Activity 1

Look at the following three extracts from texts about reality television shows. They have the same topic, but each has a different purpose.

1   Identify the **primary purpose** of each text.

2   Explain how the purpose of each text has influenced the writer's language choices.

News | Sport | Culture | Finance | Opinions | Comment |

Reality TV

The proof of our nation's love of reality TV is in the figures: more Brits (14.2 million votes in 2002) dialled a premium-rate phone number to cast their vote in the 'Big Brother' series than went to the polls in support of the victorious Labour Party at the 2005 general election (9.5 million Labour voters).

The one feature that unites the wide range of reality TV shows, and which might go some way to explaining their unrelenting popularity, is their very 'unreality'. They are contrived and exaggerated recreations of real life. As reality TV becomes widespread, the prevailing 'seen-it-all-before' viewer attitude means that the industry frequently resorts to airing larger-than-life characters undertaking increasingly extreme feats – whether this is eating live cockroaches or singing/dancing/cooking incredibly badly. Undoubtedly, the conventional limits of bad taste have been left far behind.

One example is the show 'Big Brother', which originally launched in the Netherlands in 1999 and is now part of the staple diet of hungry audiences in nearly every European country, each having adapted the show to make it their own. Contestants are carefully selected members of the public who are closeted in a 'house' for several weeks and monitored by cameras. Their activities are then broadcast (often live) on TV and viewers are invited to vote 'housemates' out of the show. The necessity to maintain interest has led to gimmicks and controversies of increasing shock-value.

Text A

Reality TV   *TV*   *Soaps*   *Celebrities*   **TV BLOG**

Why We Will Always Watch Reality TV

September 29th, 2007 by Lisa McGarry. Tags: Reality TV

The X Factor, Strictly Come Dancing, Fame Academy, American Idol, I'm a Celebrity Get me Out of Here, Big Brother, Dancing On Ice, Hell's Kitchen; if you haven't heard of any of these programmes you must have been in a coma and have just come around, you're a recluse and you live in a cave or you have been wading through a jungle in Vietnam, not yet realising that the war is over.

Reality television is at its peak at the moment and you either love it or you love it but pretend you hate it; locking yourself away on a Saturday night, in a basement somewhere, pretending to watch the Discovery Channel. So what is it that has our 21st Century Generation hooked on watching other people's lives?

Text B

Text C

The Education Forum > Curriculum Subjects > Social Sciences > Social Sciences: Changes in Society

Changes in Society: Reality Television	*Post*

Group: admin
Posts: 134
Joined: 16.12. 03
From: London

While 'Big Brother' is probably the example that most quickly springs to mind, all shows that fall into the reality TV bracket, whether they invite audience participation or not, use similar methods to promote conflict and aggression. Producers believe that this increases viewing figures and that people love to watch others arguing or being humiliated, and even find it funny. There is some evidence to support this: it reminds me of the way in which wealthy Romans used to arrange for disabled and mentally ill slaves to entertain them at dinner parties, or the way in which you could pay to watch the strange antics of patients in Bethlem Hospital in London (from which the word 'bedlam' is derived). Bethlem even hired out the patients to appear as entertainers at weddings and banquets.

Should we be worried by such programmes? After all, the participants in reality TV shows are all more than willing to take part and have even fought off stiff competition for the chance to become 'famous'. Some even come back for more of the same in order to revitalise their 'fame'.

Many texts have more than one purpose – writers are often aiming to achieve a variety of things with their writing. For example, a newspaper article might have a **primary purpose** of persuading people that reality TV shows are harmless fun, but a **secondary purpose** of entertaining and amusing its readers.

Activity ❷

Look at the two writing tasks below on the theme of reality television and the purposes listed in the box beneath.

> Write a review of a reality TV programme that has recently been broadcast for an online forum.

> Write an article giving your opinions on the subject of reality TV for a TV listings magazine.

describe	comment	amuse	inform	advise
explain	entertain	persuade	review	argue

1 For each task:

   a) decide which of the purposes given in the box might be the task's primary purpose

   b) identify any secondary purposes that the writer might also want to achieve.

2 Give reasons for each purpose you have selected.

ResultsPlus
Exam tip

The best way to revise purpose is to take the same topic and change the purpose. For instance, you could take the topic of homework in your school. You could choose to use different purposes such as comment, inform or argue.

Any text that requires you to discuss an issue, develop a point of view or convey an idea will involve developing some kind of **argument** – a connected series of ideas supported by reasons and leading towards a conclusion. For example, in a review you will need to give convincing reasons for the opinions you offer. Remember, an argument needs to:

- have a logical structure
- flag up the logic of the writer's thinking by using suitable connecting words and phrases
- lead the audience towards a conclusion
- back up ideas with reasons and evidence throughout.

You will have to generate ideas and then structure your argument quickly in the examination.

Activity 3

1 Write a paragraph of a response to each of the following tasks. Make sure you include all the elements of an argument listed above.

A | Make the case either for or against the value of reality TV programmes.

B | Give your explanation(s) for the popularity of reality shows such as Big Brother.

C | Make the case either for or against extending reality TV-style voting to political issues.

Whatever purpose you are writing for, your writing needs to appeal effectively to your readers. You can often enrich your writing style by making use of rhetorical techniques sometimes called rhetorical devices or features. They are often used to guide or influence the reader and can help to lift a dull piece of writing (especially persuasive texts), but it's important not to overuse them.

Activity 4

1 Match each rhetorical feature listed on the left with the appropriate example on the right.

Oxymoron – placing two contradictory ideas together in a single phrase	An untalented publicity-seeker makes a fool of himself and a nation watches. A celebrity no one has heard of squeals as she swallows a handful of live grubs in the jungle, and the nation watches. A collection of oddities indulge in childish antics and foul language … and the nation watches.
Tricolon or triad – a group of three words or phrases	In the 19th century people flocked to freak shows at the circus; in the 21st, they don't need to.
Irony – a humorous effect produced by implying the opposite of what is actually said	What is it that drives our endless fascination with shows like 'The X Factor?'
Parallelism – repetition of a similar phrase or sentences with just a small variation each time	If reality TV was a drug, it would be so addictive it would have been banned.
Metaphors, similes and analogies – ways of making a comparison between two things	In a recent edition of a well-known reality show we were entertained and enriched by the spectacle of a man swinging lead weights from his various body piercings. High quality entertainment indeed!
Antithesis – use of a pair of opposites or contrasts	The contestant's time on the show had definitely been the most challenging, fatiguing and incredible experience of his life.
Alliteration – words that repeat the same initial sound	Trivial, tiresome and terrible television – that's how some critics describe the new generation of reality TV shows.
Rhetorical question – a question that does not require an answer	The reality 'talent' shows feature the hopeful, the hopeless, and those beyond hope altogether.
Hyperbole – deliberate exaggeration for effect	Nothing is more unreal than so-called 'reality TV'.

2 Rewrite the following draft of part of an article which argues in favour of reality TV and is aimed at young adults. Use some rhetorical techniques of your choice to make it more effective.

Many people are worried about the number of 'reality' shows on television. Some people think they are degrading. They seem to exploit the volunteers who participate in them by humiliating them in various ways. They seem to encourage the pursuit of 'celebrity' at all costs. The viewers are invited to enjoy and find amusement in this.

However, there are different kinds of reality show. Not all of them show inadequate people making fools of themselves and being exploited. Some of the 'talent' shows may inspire us to try singing, dancing or whatever for ourselves. We may be moved by the human stories of triumph and despair they enact. There is nothing wrong with this.

So it would be wrong to condemn all Reality TV. It is human nature for human beings to take an interest in the doings of fellow humans. This is why soap operas are so popular. When we know we are watching 'reality' and not just something made up by a scriptwriter it is much more interesting.

2 Audience

This lesson will help you to...

→ achieve the right style and register for your given audience

When deciding on the content and style of your writing in the examination, you will need to think about the **audience** for your text. Sometimes it is helpful to picture someone who might be one of your readers in front of you as you write. Here are some of the questions you need to ask yourself about your readers:

- How much do they already know about the topic you are writing about?
- Which aspects of the topic would they be most interested in?
- What attitudes do you think they will have towards the topic?
- What is the most appropriate register of language to use when writing for them?

Activity 1

1 Below are examples of examination-style tasks. For each one:

a) decide who the audience is

b) briefly answer the four questions given above to establish what you need to do to write for these audiences.

A | Write an article for a local information guide recommending interesting places for young people to visit and things for them to do in your area.

B | Write an article for your school website focusing on the best things about your school.

C | Write a review in a lifestyle magazine of the benefits and drawbacks of modern technology.

D | Write a report for your local council suggesting some changes you would like to see in your area.

E | Write the script for a talk to your fellow students about alcohol-related issues.

F | Write a letter to your local newspaper about the need for more leisure facilities for young people.

It is important to match your **style** and **register** to your audience. To do this you need to develop the range of styles you can use and be versatile enough to be able to express the same idea in several different ways, depending on who you are writing for. It is helpful to think of the range of possible registers as a spectrum, from colloquial to very formal with lots of different options in between. Remember not to overuse very colloquial or very formal language in your writing.

Activity 2

Look at the three sentences below that could appear in a guide to your local area.

1 Rewrite each one in the appropriate style and register for each of these audiences:

a) Young people who are visiting the area to study

b) Families who come to the area on holiday.

> People who enjoy sport can visit the new sports centre and swimming pool or watch Premier League football at the local stadium.

> **Visitors can browse a wide range of shops and take advantage of bars, pubs, cafes and restaurants to suit every taste and budget.**

> People who prefer outdoor activities can go walking in the nearby Cheviot Hills and enjoy the unspoilt landscape.

Results Plus
Watch out!

When writing for people of your own age it is still important to write accurately. Avoid the language of text/SMS messages and the overuse of slang. A lively and jokey style is much better than too many incomplete sentences and words that your examiner might not recognise!

Activity 3

Look at the short text below about facilities for young people in the writer's local area.

> There are few facilities for young people in the area. In summer the local sports field is available but there really is not any suitable indoor venue in the winter months. The Community Centre has a number of activities but more senior citizens than young people are attracted to these. We need a decent all-weather sports centre, perhaps with some kind of cafe/coffee bar attached.

1 Rewrite the text for each of the different audiences listed below. Think about alternative words and phrases for each of those highlighted in the text – for example, would you use the phrase 'young people' in a website for teenagers?

a) An article on a website visited mainly by teenagers.

b) A report to officials at the local council.

c) A letter to a friend you met on holiday who lives elsewhere.

3 Writing in a given form

This lesson will help you to...

→ write in an appropriate form and genre

Your task in the examination will specify the form for your writing, which could include an article, a review, a speech, a report, a leaflet or a letter. To achieve the highest grades you will need to show that you can use the appropriate conventions for the form in which you are writing in examination conditions.

Activity 1

1 Remind yourself of the story of *Goldilocks and the Three Bears*.

2 Write two of the following texts, basing your ideas on the Goldilocks story.

Results Plus

Watch out!

Be careful that you only write the *text* in the form you have been given. Although newspaper articles are often written in columns and include pictures, don't try to create these or any other features relating to the layout of your form of writing.

Informative leaflet

Write the text for an informative leaflet to be produced for visitors to the wood, including warnings about the various dangers.
Conventions:
• Introductory page; information given in small chunks
• Body text in short paragraphs
• Bullets to break down key points

Report

Write a report of the Goldilocks incident following an Official Enquiry.
Conventions:
• Headings and subheadings
• Formal register
• Factual details
• No sensational language
• Quotes from witnesses

Magazine article

Write a magazine article about Goldilocks for a celebrity magazine.
Conventions:
• Headings and subheadings
• Focus on personal experiences, relationships and emotions
• Mixture of journalistic comment and interview quotes
• May include text boxes/panels for key facts, etc.

Review

Write a review of the Bear family's choice of breakfast food and interior furnishing for *Good Housekeeping* magazine.
Conventions:
• Mixture of description, information and opinions
• May follow a 'narrative' pattern – follows the sequence of the story

Script

Write the script for a talk given by the Bear family to other woods-dwellers on the subject 'Our morning from Hell - lessons in home security'.
Conventions:
• Script layout – speaker and text
• Suggestions for use of visual aids (pictures, slides) and/or sounds and music
• May include some informal touches

Letter

Write the letter that Mr Bear might write to his local council reporting the incident.
Conventions:
• Formal features – address of sender and addressee
• Formal language
• Substantial, developed paragraphs
• Appropriate sign-off (*Yours sincerely* if letter is addressed to a named person; otherwise *Yours faithfully*)

Having considered the importance of the key factors of purpose, audience and form, you should now be in a good position to attempt the kind of task you will encounter in the examination. Remember that you will need to generate your ideas and plan your writing quickly in the examination so it's a good idea to practise doing this within a time limit.

Activity 2

1 Try putting all your skills so far into practice by selecting four random numbers from 1 to 6 and attempting the piece of writing required. For example, 2 – 1 – 5 – 1 would require you to write an article about interesting places to visit in your area for people of all ages in your community, conveying your opinion convincingly.

Die roll	Form	Topic	Audience	Purpose
1	Letter	Interesting places to visit/ things to do in your area	People of your own age group and background	Convey your opinion convincingly
2	Article	The best things about your school	Adult officials and professionals	Present information clearly but without too much bias
3	News report	The benefits and drawbacks of homework	Young people in Years 7 and 8	Analyse and point out the good and bad things
4	Leaflet	Changes you'd like to see in your community/area	A relevant person in a position of some authority e.g. an MP	Make a strong case
5	Official report	Issues arising from young people's consumption of alcohol	People of all ages in your community	Persuade your audience to take action of some kind
6	Review	The need for leisure facilities in your region	People of all ages who share an interest in the topic	Offer advice and guidance

2 Next write a paragraph explaining some of the choices you made when writing your text regarding content, language, style, register and vocabulary in order to fit with purpose, audience and form.

4 Generating ideas

In your examination you will have limited time to generate ideas, plan and then complete your writing. The topics you will be asked to write about in the examination are likely to be ones which you already have experience of, so you shouldn't be short of inspiration!

You need to go into the examination with a clear planning strategy. This involves spending some time at the start **mapping** and then **sequencing** your ideas effectively. Once you have made your choice of task in the examination, you need to think fast and get your thoughts down on paper. You could approach your examination task like this:

Stage 1	Close scrutiny of task – 'unpack' what it is telling you about the purpose, audience and form.
Stage 2	Work out a paragraph-by-paragraph structure, noting the main points you will include in each.

Below is an example of a student's first stage of planning in response to an examination task.

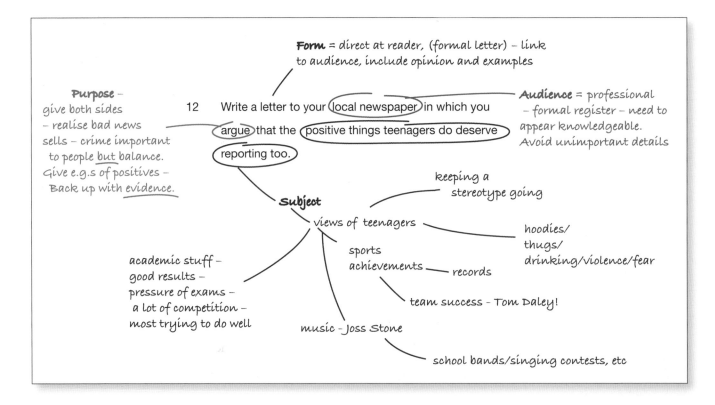

When you are aiming for the very highest grades, one of the ways in which you can make your writing stand out from the crowd is through the approach you take to the task. Sometimes it can be more interesting to adopt an unconventional or unpredictable point of view or argument. Some people call this 'thinking outside the box'. However, while originality in your ideas is a good thing, remember that it is the clarity and accuracy with which you express compelling ideas which will gain you most marks.

Activity 1

Look at the ideas suggested below for two further examination-style tasks.

> Write a review in a lifestyle magazine of the benefits and drawbacks of modern technology.

Review for lifestyle magazine

- Internet makes finding things out really easy – benefit
- Information on the internet is not always reliable – drawback
- Many jobs now done easily/quickly by computers – benefit
- People may lose their jobs as a result – drawback
- SMS and email allow us to keep in touch all the time - benefit and drawback

> Write a report for your local council suggesting some changes you would like to see in your area.

Report for local council

- Create new sports and community facilities for young people
- Encourage more businesses and shops to set up in the area
- Ban traffic and create pedestrian-friendly environment
- Sell under-used sports fields for housing development
- Demolish ugly and derelict buildings

1 For each text, identify one idea that is quite predictable and one idea that is a more unusual or creative approach to the topic, suggesting what exactly makes it more interesting.

ResultsPlus
Exam tip

Try to make your writing as interesting as possible. Your examiner will reward interesting ideas that are well expressed.

Activity 2

Look at the two examination-style tasks below.

A
> Write an article for a local information guide recommending interesting places for young people to visit and things for them to do in your area.

B
> Write an article for your school website focusing on the best things about your school.

1 Identify the audience, purpose and form of the writing required for each of the two tasks.

2 For each task, give yourself no more than five minutes to brainstorm ideas for what you could write about. Remember to think about which aspects of the topic would appeal to the audience specified in the task and what kind of ideas will be most original. You might find it helpful to use the same style of spider diagram as shown opposite.

5 Planning

This lesson will help you to...

→ **plan your writing**
→ **create a clear and effective structure**

To obtain the highest grades in the examination, you will need to show evidence of your planning in the way you have organised your ideas, sequenced them logically and written in well-controlled paragraphs.

Once you are satisfied that you have completed the first stage of generating ideas and have the basic points you need for your writing in the examination, you should move on to the second stage and organise these into a sequence. In order to do this you will need to think about the following questions relating to audience, purpose and form:

- What will you start with? What will grab your audience's attention?
- Is there any kind of 'narrative' involved? If so, should you structure your writing in a chronological sequence?
- Is there an argument involved? If so, how will you lead your audience from point to point?
- Will you organise your ideas into paragraphs by topic and theme? If so, what is the most logical path through these ideas?
- What impact do you want your ending to have on your audience?

The table below shows some suggested ways of structuring ideas, depending on purpose.

Type of structure	Chronological sequence	Balanced overview	Argument	Information
Sequence of ideas in structure	What happened first ↓ Events that followed ↓ Final event	Overview of topic ↓ Points for ↓ Points against ↓ Conclusion	Overview of topic and introduce conclusion ↓ Give reasons for conclusion and evidence in support of this (and perhaps reasons for dismissing the counter- arguments) ↓ Restate conclusion	Summary of key points/issues ↓ Expansion of key points ↓ Restate key points with summary
Advantage of each type of structure	Useful for tasks which involve an aspect of **narrative**, or storytelling	Useful for **discussions** of controversial topics where you are asked to review different points of view	Useful where you are asked to make a case or an **argument** in favour of a particular point of view	Useful for **articles** where you try to grab the attention of readers in the opening paragraph

You could use a flow chart including key headings and bullet points to summarise the main ideas you will include in each section or paragraph.

The diagram below shows a student's chosen structure for a letter to a local newspaper about reporting on teenagers (the task on page 102). They have chosen to use a sequence of ideas which is effective in putting forward their argument.

Setting out point of view — current slant on reporting (crime and negative issues connected with teenagers) may sell but as a young person myself I feel this is biased. A lot of evidence to support my view.

↓

My first hand experience — working hard at school, pressure of exams, lots of competition, most teenagers would like to do well

↓

Not only academic — sporting achievements in and out of school, music, theatre, charity and environmental work

↓

Teenage role models — Joss Stone, Tom Daley, contributing to raising Britain's profile on a world stage

↓

Teenagers who are violent/drink/commit crimes the exception to the rule. Reacting to the pressure around them, often created by adults. Negative reporting needs to become more focused on how positive action can be taken to help them.

↓

Formal ending, appealing directly to the editor. Reporting only the negative aspects of teenage life will continue the stereotype of thugs/hoodies and only make the problems worse. Newspaper has a responsibility to highlight the strengths of future adults in society.

Activity ❶

1 Decide on a structure for the ideas you mapped for one of the tasks in Activity 2 on page 103. Create a flow chart to show this.

2 Write a paragraph to explain how you have sequenced your ideas and why.

6 Effective openings

This lesson will help you to...

→ construct effective and attention-grabbing openings

Before you begin your writing in the examination, you need to ask yourself what impact you want to achieve in the opening lines of your writing. Here are some techniques for creating an arresting opening to your text, depending on the nature of your audience, purpose and form:

- Asking a provocative question – *What is the best way of grabbing your audience's attention?*

- Addressing the audience directly – *When you are faced with a writing task, the first question you ask yourself is – 'Where do I begin?'*

- Using shock tactics – *What a load of rubbish! Is that what you want your readers to think after reading your first sentence?*

- Focusing on a human interest angle – *Alison Johnson was in agony. She felt her pulse racing and the cold sweat of panic rising as she struggled to form the words of her first sentence…*

- Providing a dramatic, narrative summary of what, where and when – *GCSE student Alison Johnson, 16, yesterday produced the most dramatic opening sentence in the history of English examinations.*

- Creating an element of suspense – *The pen was poised. The words were forming in her head. This was it. The first sentence. The bait that would either hook the readers or leave them cold. What was it to be?*

ResultsPlus

Watch out!

The examiner will be influenced by your first paragraph. When you have finished writing go back to the beginning and make sure you started powerfully and not lazily.

Activity 1

Below are some possible openings for the following writing task:

> **Write a review of the past year in the life of your school or college.**

1   In each case briefly explain what makes it an effective opening.

A 'It has been a year of ups and downs.' This was the verdict of Head Teacher Mr Andrew Mackenzie on the most recent year in the life of Newtown Community College.

B 95 students achieved five or more good GCSEs and two out of three Newtown students achieved the top GCSE grades this year.

C What a year!

D To say this year has been a roller-coaster for Newtown Community College would be an understatement. It has been the Blackpool Big One, Nemesis and Log Flume all rolled into one.

Activity 2

Your choice of opening will depend on the nature of the task, and what you are trying to achieve. Look at this writing task:

> Write the text for a talk you might give to your fellow students on the subject of a favourite interest, pastime or hobby.

1 Consider the following openings for the task. Place them in rank order of preference, suggesting the reasons for your preference.

A
> "Brilliant. It has given me so much confidence, I've made lots of new friends, I've had a great laugh and I've learned a lot of general knowledge along the way." Not my words, but those of a friend who joined the school debating society last year.

B
> Last year more than 200 students came along to our five debates — they can't all be wrong.

C
> Arguments. Controversy. Conflict. All parts of everyday life, aren't they?

D
> Taking part in your first debate is a bit like becoming a fighter pilot…You don't know which direction your next attack is coming from and unless you keep your wits about you you'll end up getting shot down in flames.

Activity 3

Look at the writing task below.

> Write an article for your school/college magazine with the title: 'Is homework necessary?'

1 Experiment with writing an opening paragraph by trying two different techniques which you think might be effective.

2 Decide which of your two openings would be more effective, and say why.

7 Linking paragraphs

This lesson will help you to...

→ create a fluently written text

→ 'signpost' your writing for your readers

Your writing in the examination needs to flow from one paragraph to another in a logical way. If you have planned your writing successfully, you should already know the journey you hope to take your reader on. Now you just need to point the reader in the right direction from time to time. To do this you can use a variety of **cohesive devices**. Here's a reminder of some of these techniques:

*   Use **headings** and **subheadings**, if appropriate for the form you are writing in, to show the organisation of ideas in your text.
*   Use **linking words and phrases** regularly to introduce new sentences and paragraphs.
*   From time to time '**announce**' what is coming next e.g. 'as we'll see' and **refer back** to what has gone before e.g. 'as we saw'.
*   Make a **reference in your final sentence to something you said in your first** – possibly by repeating a phrase or answering the question you asked.

This 'signposting' is also important within individual paragraphs. A well-written paragraph will usually begin with a topic sentence. This announces the main subject of the paragraph before you go on to develop the idea or illustrate it with examples and quotations. As with the whole text, each paragraph should have a logical structure and will include conjunctive words and phrases like 'so' or 'in addition'. It might even have some sort of concluding paragraph to summarise the points made within it.

A clear topic sentence that defines the subject of the paragraph and normally links to the previous paragraph

The main body of the paragraph will develop, explain or exemplify the topic

> Some parents and theorists think that school holidays are too long and argue that it takes students a while to get back into 'learning mode' after the break.
> There is evidence to suggest that students dip at the start of each year and take a little time to progress further than they were before. Therefore, the sooner they get back into learning mode, the sooner they can begin achieving again.

Synonyms to lend variety to writing

Discourse marker to signpost conclusion of paragraph topic

Reinforcement of key words or phrases through repetition

Textual 'signposts' come in many forms, depending on the level of formality you think is suitable for your task. They are a way of guiding your readers through the text.

Activity 1

Look at the ideas in the table below.

1 Think of as many words and phrases as possible to 'signpost' these ideas in different kinds of text. One example of each has been provided to get you started.

Message to reader	Textual signposts
What's coming next is another example of what I've just been telling you	Moreover…
What's coming next is an example of what I've just said	For instance…
The next point follows logically from the one before	As a consequence…
Look out – this is an important bit!	It is clear that…
What's coming up is the next in a series of related ideas	Secondly…
I'm going to introduce a contrasting idea here	However…
Get ready – here comes my conclusion	Inevitably…
This is what is coming up next	In today's programme…
Remember what I was talking about before?	As we saw earlier…

As you write, you need to ensure that you include signposts such as these to prevent your writing becoming a series of unconnected points. You want your writing to be fluent and cohesive.

Activity 2

Re-read the paragraph about school holidays on page 108.

1 Write a paragraph which follows on from this one and explores the view that school holidays should be extended. Make sure you have a clear topic sentence and go on to develop your ideas. Guide your reader through the text by using appropriate cohesive devices.

Activity 3

Read the newspaper article below which has been written by a student in response to the following task:

> A neighbourhood school plans to build an all-weather sports pitch on one of its fields but has encountered opposition to the plan from local residents at a recent public meeting. Produce an article for a local newspaper that reviews the controversy.

1 Improve the article by making the changes and additions suggested below.

1 Create a suitably punchy headline.

2 Insert a topic sentence that refers more directly to the public meeting mentioned in the opening and also signposts what the new paragraph is all about.

3 Add a linking word or phrase that signposts 'here is another reason'.

4 Add a suitable linking word.

5 Insert a one-word subheading here which summarises the content of the next paragraph.

6 Add an opening 'topic' sentence to this paragraph that also links back to the previous one.

7–9 Signpost this list of objections by numbering them in some way.

10 Insert a word or phrase that 'signposts' that a conclusion is coming.

---

1 ....

A local school's plans for an all-weather sports pitch have run into fierce opposition from local residents. At a public meeting last night attended by over 100 residents, Norton High School Head Teacher Janet Newman faced a barrage of objections from neighbours concerned about the impact of the proposed pitch on the local community.

2 .... The school's case for building the pitch is a strong one. In the current drive to encourage young people to adopt healthy lifestyles, an all-weather facility would enable the school not only to run its own sporting activities throughout the year but also to open the pitch for community use in the evenings. 3 .... the days of endless postponements of games due to waterlogged pitches would be over. 4 .... at last night's meeting, Mrs Newman went on to argue that far from having a negative impact on the neighbourhood, the pitch would enhance the amenities of the area and provide a much-needed facility for local youngsters that would help keep them off the streets and out of trouble.

5 ....

6 ....The local residents clearly have their own reasons to resist the plan. 7 .... there is the physical impact of the pitch on the immediate environment. The high security fences are unattractive and high-powered floodlights shining long into the night would be a considerable nuisance to those living nearby. 8 .... neighbours fear the impact of increased traffic caused by visitors coming back and forth to use the pitch in what is already a densely populated area with scarce parking. The 9 .... objection is that the facility may attract groups of youths and prove to be a magnet for trouble of various kinds.

10 .... there is a need for communication and compromise between both sides in the dispute. The shortage of sporting facilities for young people in the area needs to be addressed, at the same time as satisfying the reasonable objections of residents.

Here is an example of an examination question you could be expected to answer. You will be expected to write a letter with paragraphs that link together effectively.

> Write a letter to students in which you persuade them that a trip in term time would be a good idea or would not be a good idea.
>
> (24 marks)

Activity 4

Write two paragraphs of the letter to students. Focus on effectively linking paragraphs together.

You should spend 20 minutes on this task.

ResultsPlus
Self assessment

Before you complete this self-assessment activity, you might like to read some sample answers to this task on the following pages (112-113).

1 **Check your answer to Activity 4:**

- Did you use words to connect ideas across paragraphs?
- Did you use questions to help set up ideas which you later go on to answer?
- Did you create a structure where the opening links directly to the ending?

2 **Now try to decide which Band your answer to Activity 4 would fit into by applying the mark scheme opposite. You will need to be careful and precise in your marking.**

Higher Tier Band 3
- text structure is securely organised and well judged
- effective use of cohesive devices between and within paragraphs

Higher Tier Band 4
- text structure is assured, with sophisticated control of structure
- skilfully sustained paragraphs and effective use of cohesive devices

Higher Tier Band 5
- organisation is convincing, with sophisticated control of structure
- skilfully sustained paragraphs and effective use of cohesive devices

Maximise your marks

Write two paragraphs of the letter to students in which you persuade them that a trip in term time would be a good idea or would not be a good idea. You should focus on the effective linking of paragraphs.

Here are three student answers to the letter task on page 111. Read the answers together with the examiner comments and then complete the activity at the bottom of page 113.

Student 1 – Extract typical of a grade (B) answer

This opening phrase shows that the writer has an idea of the whole text as they have clearly thought about how this paragraph will link to the others.

> The main reason for a trip abroad is to be with your friends and have a good time whilst you are away. You will have an informal relationship with the dedicated staff and other pupils. Because you see these people in a new light it opens up the possibility of new ideas. Therefore, travel abroad will make you more and more tolerant to the ideas and friendship of others.
>
> Another reason for a trip abroad is the chance to learn. For instance, if you travel to places like France and Belgium you may want to visit the World War graves. This would be useful for a younger generation, as it will teach them the great sacrifices that the soldiers made for us to be free.

Good use of cohesive devices within paragraphs.

Use of similar paragraph opening to show links between the paragraphs.

Examiner summary

This part of the answer is typical of a grade B performance. The use of the phrase 'The main reason' persuades the reader that Student 1 has an idea what the whole of the text will be. This means that the structure of the writing is likely to be logical. The use of the phrase 'Another reason' is effective as the reader knows that each paragraph will offer reasons to support travel abroad. The use of the word 'therefore' within the paragraph shows the student can use discourse markers within paragraphs, linking ideas throughout.

Student 2 – Extract typical of a grade (A) answer

Important repetition of key words from the previous paragraph means the student can avoid overuse of discourse markers that can make writing sound quite dry.

> Why is travel abroad in school time such a controversial issue? Educationalists suggest that the lost time in the classroom can impact on students' performance in the examination because there is a period afterwards when the student has to catch up.
>
> Examination preparation cannot be the only type of learning that goes on in the world. What a shallow world we live in if the only way to find out about people, places, culture and customs is through the talk and chalk of a teacher. It is so important to get out into the world and experience it for ourselves. This is the most powerful learning experience there is.

Good use of a question to set up the issue for the reader.

Examiner summary

This part of the answer is typical of a grade A performance. The student has decided on a 'for and against' structure. They effectively use a question as a cohesive device – introducing the reader to the topic of the paragraph. The second paragraph avoids using discourse markers such as "however" which can sometimes make writing sound dry. Instead they present an alternative perspective using a simple statement. This lends the writing a confident tone, and the reader is convinced the writer knows where they are going.

A strong statement of the writer's point of view will likely be revisited in the final paragraph, once the justification of this statement has been presented in the rest of the response.

Travel abroad is an important educational experience as students are immersed in the culture and traditions of different countries. This valuable time away from the classroom brings everything learnt from the text book into sharp focus. The Minister for Schools, John Edwards, noted that: "Teenagers who had experienced travel abroad are 34% more likely to achieve the standard of 5 A* – C grades required by government standards."

Opposition groups claim that the time out of the classroom actually impacts negatively on the experience of students. Young people not only miss the lessons whilst they are away but also struggle to catch up once they return. But, surely this is a temporary blip? NUT union leader Tom Jerward claims not: "The insecurity and loss of confidence caused by time away is the most damaging factor in the underachievement of teenagers." I would have thought the throwing of chairs and random swearing offered more of a challenge myself!

Specific examples are used to support the point being made

Examiner summary

This part of the answer is typical of a grade A* performance. The student has opted for a logical structure. They have begun their piece with a strong statement of belief. They then offer a counter-argument. The alternative viewpoints in this second paragraph are handled well, using questions to undermine the opposing argument. The way they set up the piece in the first paragraph suggests the conclusion will focus on how they have proved this statement of belief to be true.

ResultsPlus
Build better answers

Move from a Grade B to a Grade A

In this part of the answer you need to begin to use more advanced cohesive devices to move between ideas. Student 1's response was well structured and ideas were clearly set out. The use of discourse markers helped to move the reader through the piece. Student 2 sounded more interesting because they used questions and repeated word patterns between paragraphs to ensure the piece was well structured.

Aim for a Grade A*

In this part of the answer you need to use a more complex structure from the start. Student 2 opted for a 'for and against' structure, which meant that moving between paragraphs only required them to signal to the reader which side they were now considering. Student 3 handled both sides of the argument at the same time, using counter-argument. They used questions as a cohesive device, to signal to the reader how these points did not undermine the original statement made.

Putting it into practice

1 **Write an argument for the school website arguing for or against school uniform. Try using counter-argument. Make sure you structure your writing carefully.**

8 Choosing vocabulary

ResultsPlus
Build better answers

Look at this examination question:
Write a letter to your teacher advising them on the right approach to bullying.

■ A Higher Tier Band 3 answer **will include well-chosen vocabulary, using words that are appropriate** from simple ones such as 'wrong' to powerful ones such as 'horrific', depending on the context.

● A Higher Tier Band 4 answer **will include a fairly extensive vocabulary, consistently** selecting words that match the intended audience such as 'dehumanising' and 'self-esteem.'

▲ A Higher Tier Band 5 answer **will include an extensive vocabulary.** It will be mature using a **vocabulary** that a teacher would expect a colleague to use when exploring practice in a school.

The words you choose to use in your writing are the basic building blocks of your text – it is important to find the right words for the right context and to use them to say exactly what you mean.

Aspects of vocabulary choice include:

• achieving the right level of formality or informality for the audience, purpose and form

• conveying your meanings precisely

• choosing words with the right **connotations**

• using words and phrases in an original way.

As you brainstorm your ideas in response to the examination task, jot down the kinds of vocabulary that are going to be useful. To avoid repetition in your writing, you will need to think of a variety of words for similar or related ideas linked to the subject of your task.

Activity ①   Look at this writing task:

> **Write an article for your school magazine with the title 'The school of the future'.**

The table below shows a set of ideas you might want to cover in your response to this task.

Education	curriculum subjects discipline resources
School building	school college corridor library
The past (19th/20th century)	tradition Victorian
The future	advancement technology

1 For each idea listed on the left, spend a few minutes – with or without the help of a thesaurus – thinking of as many potentially useful words as you can. A few have been suggested to get you started.

Your choice of vocabulary depends on audience, purpose and form. The school magazine task above implies a broad adult and student audience with an interest in educational issues, so you can aim for a mature and expressive range of vocabulary that doesn't 'talk down' to its audience and includes some appropriate specialised terms.

Activity 2

Look at this draft response to the school magazine task from Activity 1, in which there are some vocabulary choices still to be made. Some choices require you to make decisions about style, and some relate to subtle connotations of words.

1 Using a dictionary and thesaurus if necessary, make your vocabulary choices, either from the options provided or using your own alternative. Make a note of the reasons for your choices and the difference they make to the impact of your text.

1 old/traditional/ decrepit/ outmoded?

3 building/design/ architecture/ construction?

7 straight/rigid/ disciplined/ geometric?

8 controlled/ supervised/ruled/ policed?

12 read/pored over/devoured/ studied?

13 forefathers/ ancestors/ predecessors/ equivalents?

14 sceptical/ inquisitive/quick-minded?

17 given/fed/ instilled with?

18 our ideal/Utopia/ perfection?

2 received/inherited/ taken on?

4 showed/reflected/ were suitable for?

5 world/agenda/ curriculum?

6 quiet/passive/ receptive/docile?

9 disciplinarian/ strict/bad/ unyielding?

10 separate/bleak/ cell-like?

11 a morgue/a church/a grave?

15 robots/slaves/ automata?

16 reproduce/ regurgitate/repeat?

The school of the future will be a very different place from the 1 buildings we have 2 from the past. The world of education is changing fast and the school of tomorrow will reflect these changes.

The 3 of the schools of the past 4 an educational 5 very different from today's. Traditional subjects — English, Maths, Science and so on — were taught by teachers 'from the front'. Pupils were expected to be 6 and well-behaved, so sat in 7 rows which were 8 by 9 teachers. The school building, which consisted of many 10 classrooms, reflected the way pupils themselves were sorted into classes. The Library was a large book-lined room as silent as 11 where students 12 books. Until very recently, most school buildings reflected these values in their design.

In the 21st century we don't need to be sitting in classrooms to learn. With constant access to online educational resources, we can learn anywhere, at any time. The pupils of today are not as passive — or as silent — as our Victorian 13. The modern world needs confident, articulate, sociable and 14 young people with initiative, not well-behaved 15 programmed unthinkingly to 16 information they have been 17 by teachers. As a result a new generation of school buildings has started to appear. What would the perfect school of the 21st century actually look like? We may never achieve 18 but we can at least start to dream...

9 Punctuation choices

This lesson will help you to...

→ use the full range of punctuation effectively

The two aspects of punctuation you need to practise as you approach the examination are:

- getting the basics right – making sure your sentences are accurately punctuated with attention to detail
- using advanced punctuation for expression – using punctuation effectively to create the right tone and impact.

Activity 1

Look at the draft article below. It was written for teenagers to inform them about a role model the writer admires.

1 Rewrite the draft, using correct punctuation.

> What is a role model it is someone who has achieved something with their life to which the rest of us aspire this might include sportsmen or women such as Paula Radcliffe, pop stars such as Paolo Nutini or politicians such as Barack Obama to name just a few but for many people this is not enough a role model should also be an example of some of the qualities that we would want to emulate they may have shown heroism or courage or determination in the face of setbacks or simply devoted their lives to the service of others.
>
> Young people certainly need people to look up to if the most influential people in their lives are the trivial inadequate and insignificant Big Brother famous-for-fifteen-minutes contestants the media inflate into celebrities or worse their local gang leaders role models must be close enough to allow young people to identify with them but worthy of great respect

Once you are confident you are using punctuation accurately, you can go on to use punctuation to create a particular tone and achieve a specific effect. Punctuation that will show your control of the full range includes:

– dash	Can introduce a touch of suspense and drama – makes us wait for the last part of a sentence.
; semi-colon	Can link two whole sentences where the ideas in each are balanced or complementary or else can join together a series of linked phrases to create more of a break than a simple comma.
: colon	Can link two whole sentences where the ideas in the first sentence lead to those in the second. Can also be used to introduce a list.
! exclamation mark	Can make the text 'shout'! Or express a note of surprise, even irony!
... ellipsis	Can imply a continuation of a list or an idea... and invite reflection.
? question mark	The question – useful for provoking or involving your reader, isn't it?
() parenthesis	Useful for introducing side-comments (if you need to make them!) on the topic of the sentence.

Activity ②

Study the draft below of the closing paragraphs of the article about role models, and look at the punctuation options suggested in the annotations.

1   Make your choices, and make a note of your reasons.

1 Should this be a question or not?

2 Here, choose between dashes or parentheses to separate off the list of examples. Remember to insert a pair of these in the appropriate places.

3 Here, choose between a comma and a dash to introduce 'our own family'.

Why do people need role models? **1** Young people need role models for many reasons. We look to our idols to set an example of what we can achieve, as models of good behaviour, as sources of wisdom and advice. Most people think of role models as celebrities of one kind or another **2** musicians, singers, film stars, politicians but in some ways the most important role models are the people closest to our everyday lives **3** our own family.

Our family should be the place where we find our first role models. These might be our mums, dads, grandparents, or older brothers and sisters. These people can be hugely influential in shaping the kinds of people we grow up to be **4** for good or ill **5**. From them we derive our values and our beliefs about what is good and bad, important or not, in life **6**. From my own mum and dad I learned very early that the pursuit of money for its own sake was much less important than doing the right thing and being honest in both work and play.

My parents weren't terribly **7** successful, but they brought up three children (me included!) to be decent, happy and hard-working adults. They must have done something right **8**.

4 Here, choose between using a dash or comma before 'for good or ill'.

5 Full stop here – or exclamation mark?

6 Full stop or semi-colon here?

7 Consider using inverted commas around the word 'successful' to suggest that the definition of this word is open to interpretation.

8 The end of the piece. Consider full stop, exclamation mark or ellipsis.

Activity ③

1 Write your own paragraph about someone you see as a role model. Think about how you could use punctuation to achieve your desired tone and impact by referring to the list on the opposite page.

10 Checking and editing

This lesson will help you to...

→ check your work carefully for avoidable errors

→ achieve a high standard of technical accuracy in your writing

To obtain a top Band in your examination, your work must demonstrate a high level of technical accuracy and stylistic control. Plan your time to allow a few minutes to check for errors.

Activity ❶

Study the list of common errors below.

1 **Decide which ones you are most likely to make under pressure and make sure you look out for them in your work.**

Paragraphing	Failure to organise writing into paragraphs – use formal spacing with each paragraph (except the first one) indented a little.
Homophonic and other common spelling errors	Confusion of **homophones** – words which sound the same but are spelt differently – e.g. *their/there, practice/practise*. Misspellings of *independent, definitely, necessary, parallel, received, quite/quiet*.
Incorrect use of commas	Relying on commas to link whole sentences rather than using conjunctions or the semi-colon, colon or dash.
Sentences running out of control	Sentences going on for too long when your thoughts run out of control.
Missing or redundant apostrophes	Omitting apostrophes where required – *Michaels face was smeared with tears* – or using them where they aren't – *Two pounds of tomato's*. The tricky issue of *its* and *it's*: *it's = it is*, NOT *belonging to it*; *its = belonging to it*.
Punctuation of speech	Punctuation at end of speech goes inside closing speech marks – *"Many students fail to pay attention to this kind of detail,"* the teacher warned. Indent/new paragraph when a different speaker is quoted.
Inappropriate personal tone	Using first person *(I, me)* and second person *(you)* in texts where this is not appropriate.
Inappropriate informality	Using language that is too colloquial or informal for the context – using regional speech/dialect where standard English is required (e.g. *I have wrote*).
Lapse into 'text' language	Including short, phonetic spellings (e.g. *u* for *you*) and failing to capitalise I.
Clumsy phrasing	Using not-quite-the-right words, or awkward phrasing.

ResultsPlus
Exam tip

It is not a good idea to check your work only in the last five minutes. Write a paragraph, then read over a paragraph. The last five minutes should be reserved for accuracy checks only such as spelling and punctuation.

When checking your work, try to read it through carefully, if you have time.

- Check for paragraphing, sentence control, punctuation, phrasing and choice of expression. Try to 'hear' the text in your head.

- Then check for basic spelling errors. It can be helpful to read the text backwards – you won't be distracted by the sense and are more likely to spot errors.

Activity 2

1 Spend two minutes checking the text below. Note any corrections you think it needs.

In the heat of the moment your thoughts may be racing ahead and you may lose control over the words coming out of your head and threw your pen onto the paper. What's more, even proffesional writers have 'blind spots' and may make different sorts of errors as they rush to complete their task so, you definately need some checking time at the end. Don't expect to spot all your errors easily though, the eye is easily fooled when we reread our own writing. So you need a systematic approach. Set out to look for particular errors that you know are your 'Achilles heel, and for misspelings, try reading your writing backwards to concentrate on words individually. Unfortunaty, even this exercise is an artificiall one, its always a lot easier to spot mistakes in writing you haven't wrote yourself. So now you've got to put this into practise by becoming your own proofreader next time you complete a peace of you're own.

Assessment practice

To the right is an example of an examination question you could be expected to answer.

As part of this question you will be expected to check and edit your work, making the best possible choices.

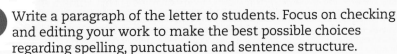

Write a letter to students in which you persuade them that a trip in term time would be a good idea or would not be a good idea.

(24 marks)

Activity 3

Write a paragraph of the letter to students. Focus on checking and editing your work to make the best possible choices regarding spelling, punctuation and sentence structure.

You should spend 10 minutes on this task.

ResultsPlus
Self assessment

Before you complete this self-assessment activity, you might like to read some sample answers to this task on the following pages (120-121).

1 Check your answer to Activity 3:

- Did you use words to connect ideas across paragraphs?
- Did you use questions to help set up ideas which you later go on to answer?
- Did you use a structure where the opening directly links to the ending?

2 Now decide which Band your answer to Activity 3 will fall into by applying the mark scheme opposite. You will need to be careful and precise in your marking.

■ Higher Tier Band 2

- spelling is almost always accurate
- sound use of full range of punctuation, helping intended effect to be created.
- a wide variety of sentences that are clearly structured.

● Higher Tier Band 3

- spelling is consistently accurate
- there is control of a range of punctuation, controlling the meaning of the text for the reader
- a convincing selection of sentence structure.

Write a paragraph of the letter to students in which you persuade them that a trip in term time would be a good idea or would not be a good idea.

Focus on checking and editing your work to make the best possible choices regarding spelling, punctuation and sentence structure.

Here are three student answers to the letter task on page 119. Read the answers together with the examiner comments around and after the answers. Then complete the activity at the bottom of page 121.

Student 1 – Extract typical of a grade (B) answer

Use of a question for effect, challenging the reader to disagree.

A clear structure, using a variety of sentences to keep the reader interested.

> If taking a holiday is good for you at that particular time, then why not take one? There are many students who are bullied in schools, so taking a break would give them time to relax without other students interfering. John Mandy, a Year 10 student from St Bernard's School in London, has been bullied for the past 2 years. In order to relieve the pressure of this abuse, he took a holiday in Majorca with his family. His father took time to talk things through with John at this time. After returning to school John found he was able to find a group of friends who accepted him.

Spelling is accurate throughout.

Examiner summary

This part of the answer is typical of a grade B performance. This student is accurate throughout and there are some good vocabulary choices. There is a use of a question for effect and the other sentences show accurate use of a range of sentence structures.

Student 2 – Extract typical of a grade (A) answer

> Returning to the classroom posed real problems for Sally Dennehy. She had loved her time in Ireland: visiting places linked to her heritage; walking along the rugged west coast... But now each hour of the day was proving a struggle. She had no real idea what any of her teachers were talking about. They assumed she knew, as the rest of the class did. It took Sally two further weeks to feel back in control of her learning. Was the trip to her homeland worth four weeks of her education in Year 11?

There are some punctuation choices that control the tone of the response.

Spelling, punctuation and sentences are entirely accurate.

Examiner summary

This part of the answer is typical of a grade A performance. The paragraph is entirely accurate, with no spelling or grammatical errors. There is control of different sentence forms, including using semi-colon to separate listed phrases in a particularly complex sentence.

Despite advanced vocabulary the spelling is consistently accurate.

It is against the law. It is really as simple as that. Legislation was brought in to protect and sanctify the education of children above all other pursuits. It is no good arguing about the cost, the richness of the cultural experience or the absolute right to control your child's life. Someone you elected decided that education within a school was paramount and holiday time (by virtue of its name) was the time for holidays. It is time to stop whining!

There is a variety of sentence forms, including simple sentences where this effect is needed. There is no over-reliance on complex sentence forms.

Examiner summary

This part of the answer is typical of a grade A* performance. The student has adopted a strong tone of voice that is controlled well through the choice of sentences. They have been confident enough in their choices to realise that complexity is not always required to achieve a very good piece of writing.

ResultsPlus
Build better answers

Move from a Grade (B) to a Grade (A)

In this part of the answer you need to increase the complexity of your choices. Both Student 1 and Student 2 are accurate. Student 2 has made choices that require far more skill than Student 1. The level of control, particularly in punctuation, means that Student 2 is more typical of an A grade response.

Aim for a Grade (A*)

In this part of the answer you need to understand that controlling the meaning of a text with sentences and punctuation doesn't always require complexity but does demand variety. Student 2 did control sentences and punctuation accurately but in some ways the pace and tone of the writing were monotonous. Student 3 understood that simple sentence construction can sometimes have a more powerful impact on the reader.

Putting it into practice

1   Write a paragraph about teachers in which you use no punctuation and simple vocabulary. Ask three friends to write out the paragraph using more sophisticated vocabulary and a variety of punctuation. Read the responses out loud and discuss the impact of the different choices.

2   Read different texts including novels, newspapers and magazines. You will encounter different sentence forms and vocabulary that will enrich your own writing.

Examination practice

Examiner's tip

This is a sample of Section B for the Unit 2 Higher Tier Examination for **GCSE English Language**.

Examiner's tip

Select one of the questions to write about. Remember to make your writing appropriate for the specified purpose, form and audience.

GCSE English Language
HIGHER TIER

SECTION B: WRITING

Answer **ONE** question in this section.

EITHER

*9   Your local council is planning some changes and has asked you to write a review of community facilities for young people.

Write a review which includes suggestions for future improvements.

(24)

OR

*10 Write an article for an information guide recommending a place of interest in the UK that might be enjoyable to visit.

(24)

TOTAL FOR SECTION B = 24 MARKS

TOTAL FOR PAPER = 64 MARKS

GCSE English
HIGHER TIER

SECTION C: WRITING

Answer EITHER Question 11 OR Question 12 in this section.

EITHER

*11 Write a magazine article for parents with the title 'What makes a good school'?

(48 marks)

OR

*12 Write a speech on the topic of 'Stress and Modern Life' to be given to a group of your peers.

(48 marks)

TOTAL FOR SECTION B = 48 MARKS

TOTAL FOR PAPER = 96 MARKS

Examiner's tip

This is a sample of Section C for the Unit 2 Higher Tier Examination for **GCSE English**.

Examiner's tip

Select one of the questions to write about. Remember to make your writing appropriate for the specified audience, purpose and form and to attempt original approaches to the task to help you gain the highest grades.

Unit 3 Creative English: Writing

This unit is a GCSE English unit. If you are taking GCSE English Language, turn to page 152 for Unit 3: Spoken Language.

The Creative English unit gives you the opportunity to develop your speaking and listening skills, study a selection of poems and produce your own piece of creative writing. This student book unit focuses on the creative writing task and helps you to develop your creative writing skills. You will read different examples of fiction writing – narratives, descriptions, monologues and scripts – and learn how to produce your own creative writing in response to a piece of stimulus material which you'll be given to spark ideas for your writing. There are lots of different stimulus materials and activities in this section of the book for you to practise with. You will see how professional writers produce effective creative writing and be shown how to try out similar techniques in your own writing. The texts and activities you will encounter as you develop these skills are all focused on helping you to achieve the best grade you can in your Unit 3 controlled assessment task.

Your assessment

This unit is a controlled assessment unit for GCSE English. You will complete **one** Creative Writing task which you will have two hours to complete. The task will be based on one of four themes: *Relationships, Clashes and Collisions, Somewhere, Anywhere,* or *Taking a Stand.* You will be given stimulus material based on the chosen theme (this could be an image, podcast or video clip) and asked to write a narrative, description, monologue or script in response to a task. You can write up to 1000 words in your response.

Your response to the task must show that you can:

✔ write clearly, effectively and imaginatively in a specific form to engage your reader

✔ make sure that you spell, punctuate and use grammar accurately and appropriately for the purpose of your writing and to achieve the desired effect.

Assessment Objectives

Your response to the writing task will be marked using these Assessment Objectives:

✔ Write clearly, effectively and imaginatively, using and adapting forms and selecting vocabulary appropriate to the task and purpose in ways that engage the reader.

✔ Organise information and ideas into structured and sequenced sentences, paragraphs and whole texts, using a variety of linguistic and structural features to support cohesion and overall coherence.

✔ Use a range of sentence structures for clarity, purpose and effect, with accurate punctuation and spelling.

This student book unit will help you to understand what these require you to do so that you can write a successful response to your controlled assessment writing task.

1 Generating ideas

For your controlled assessment creative writing task, you will be asked to write 1000 words in the form of a narrative, description, monologue or script. You will be given a piece of stimulus material to help you generate ideas. This material could be a photograph, a video or a podcast, for example. Whatever the stimulus you are given, if you ask the right questions you will be able to develop exciting and original ideas.

Activity ❶
Look at the painting below. It is by the artist Edward Hopper and is called *Nighthawks*.

1   Explore the painting by answering these questions:

   a) What is shown in the picture and where is it?

   b) What time of day or night is it?

   c) Who are the people in the picture? What are they thinking? What are they feeling? What might they be saying to each other?

   d) What has happened in the time leading up to the moment caught in the picture?

   e) What happens next?

   f) How does this picture make you feel? Try to use some of the senses – sight, sound, smell, touch and taste.

   g) What does the picture remind you of? Does it conjure up any memories of events in your life?

2   Re-read your answers to the questions. List the ideas that you like and decide how they could link together to form a piece of creative writing.

3   Decide how you would want to present your ideas in response to this stimulus: narrative, description, script, or monologue. What might be the advantages and disadvantages of each?

Another possible stimulus would be a podcast or video clip, which could include images, speech and/or music. As with an image stimulus, you should be prepared to spend time repeatedly revisiting the material, listening or watching several times.

Activity ❷

1 Listen to the podcast available on the ActiveTeach about two men attempting to cross the Atlantic in a rowing boat. Answer the questions below to create a map of ideas inspired by the podcast.

a) What visual images are suggested to you by what you hear?

b) Take two or three of these images and describe them in your own words, exploiting the senses (sight, sound, touch, taste and smell).

c) Think about the place described in the podcast. Would you like to go there? Who else might go there? Why?

d) Listen again, and make a note of any story or stories told by the piece.

e) For any of these stories, make a note of what you think might happen next.

f) Listen again to the clip, and make a note of what you learn about any characters.

g) Make notes about any factual details given in the piece. Decide what issues arising from these it might be useful or interesting to research.

h) What do the sounds or images that you have heard remind you of? Has anything similar occurred in your own life?

Three thousand miles; two guys in a wooden boat; one goal.

In a 24-foot plywood boat, with only two oars to propel them and the power in their bodies to drive them on, Stuart Turnbull and Edward Baylis will row unsupported across the Atlantic ocean in aid of Cancer Research UK.

ResultsPlus
Self assessment

Check your answer – have you:

• thought about what your overall message is going to be in your writing?

• considered how you are going to suggest this message in the language you choose?

• tested out different ideas and voices before opting for an approach in your controlled assessment?

Activity ❸

1 Now look at the stimulus that you have been given for your controlled assessment task or one of the practice tasks on page 151. Use the strategies that you have learned in this lesson to explore it and then write a paragraph explaining what ideas you would include in your writing and, if possible, what form you would write in.

2 Narrative writing

This lesson will help you to...

→ understand different ways to structure your writing

To write a narrative in response to your controlled assessment task, you will first need to devise a **plot**. A plot will usually involve these four stages:

| A **situation** and **character(s)** are briefly sketched | → | A **problem** or **complication** is introduced | → | Some kind of **crisis** or **conflict** develops | → | The crisis is **resolved**, or left **unresolved** |

Your piece of writing must be no longer than 1000 words, so it is important to create a plot that is not too complex. Focus on creating an interesting character within a believable situation.

Look at this example of a controlled assessment task.

> Look at the image on the left. Write a text which explores EITHER the events leading up to this moment OR the events which directly follow this moment.

Below is one student's outline plan for a narrative plot in response to the task.

Situation and characters	A boy discovers that his mother, who abandoned him when he was a baby, has returned to the town where he lives.
Complication or problem	His father doesn't want him to seek out his mother.
Crisis	He finds his mother, but she slams the door in his face. He is upset and runs away, not looking where he is going, and is hit by a car.
Resolution	His mother feels terrible and comes to visit him in hospital. She promises not to run away again.

ResultsPlus
Controlled assessment tip

Choose a situation or setting for your narrative that you have experience of. Using one from a film or novel may make your writing unbelievable or clichéd.

Activity ❶

Now look at the image on the right

1 Answering the same sample controlled assessment task, outline three different plots that could be developed from this stimulus. In each case, decide what the four key stages of your plot would be.

2 Now decide which of the three plots you have outlined offers the most potential and is achievable in the word limit of 1000 words.

Whatever storyline you choose, there are many different ways of telling it. One important decision you have to make is the order in which to tell the events and how to hook in your readers at the start: in other words, the **narrative structure**. There are two basic options:

- Start at the beginning, and narrate the events in the order in which they take place.

- Start at a point in the middle, or at the end, and use flashback (or flash forward) to take readers back (or forward) in time.

Activity ②

Below are some possible openings to the example plot given opposite. The response to the task has been given the title 'The Return'.

1 **Study each type of opening and note down its advantages and disadvantages. What makes each one more or less effective?**

Starts at the beginning with dialogue

"I'm telling you, I saw her, clear as day!" Aunt Linda hissed.
"Shh," whispered Dad, "the lad will hear you." Through the crack in the door I could see his anguished face. I was trying to stay quiet, but my mind was racing – could they really be talking about my mother?

Starts at the beginning with narrative/description

It was snowing the day I found out about my mother. I remember sitting in my bedroom that morning, watching the huge flakes floating gently down from the low, heavy sky and feeling annoyed that I couldn't go to football practice. Of course, I had no idea about Mum then. If it hadn't been snowing, if I had gone to football, I might never have found out.

Starts at the climax of story

"Sorry," she said coldly, "you must be mistaken." Her words rang in my ears like thunder. I didn't know where to go, what to do, I just had to get away. Running, I started out into the road and then…
A noise, my own breath gasping, and a moment later a terrible pain. Then everything went black, like someone had drawn the curtains on the world.

Starts at the very end of story

The doctors were at the foot of my bed, talking to my father, but they sounded far away, as if they were at the bottom of the sea or maybe on the moon. My leg was broken, but at that moment I didn't care. The only thing that mattered was that Mum was just beyond that wall, sitting in the waiting room drinking horrible coffee from the machine. And I knew she would never go away again.

Activity 3

Return to the narrative plot you chose in Activity 1.

1   Decide on the structure you intend to use – will you start at the beginning or at some other point in the story?

2   Sketch out the structure of your writing paragraph by paragraph using a flow chart like this:

> **Paragraph 1**
> Start in middle with 'crisis' — mother denies the boy, he runs off and is hit by a car.

> **Paragraph 2**
> Flashback to beginning of the day — description to set the scene of the day.

> **Paragraph 3**
> Background to the story — overheard conversation between father and aunt. The boy follows his aunt and finds out where his mother lives.

> **Paragraph 4**
> Return to moment before boy meets mother. Focus on boy's feelings as he is knocking on the front door.

> **Paragraph 3**
> In the hospital. Mother visits boy and reveals how guilty she feels and says she loves him. The boy is guarded with his mother. Finish with private thoughts of the boy in the hospital bed, secretly overjoyed that she has come to visit him.

ResultsPlus
Controlled assessment tip

It is a good idea to stick to small events, a brief time frame and just a few characters within your controlled assessment task. This will allow you to more easily use effective, powerful language, develop plot and characterisation.

If you move forward or back in your story, you will need to be careful about the **tense** that you use. Check your writing carefully to ensure that you have used the correct forms of the verbs in each section. For more information on tenses, look at page 145.

One of the most important choices you will make as a writer is to decide on the **viewpoint** of your piece.

- In a **third-person narrative**, the narrator stands above and outside the story. All the characters are referred to as 'he', 'she', 'they' and so on. This **'omniscient'** narrator knows everything about all of the characters and can see into their minds, choosing what to reveal to the readers at any time. The narrative can also easily move between different times and places so that the reader can experience all the meaningful events directly.

- A **first-person narrative** tells the story from the point of view of one of the characters who is involved in the events. The narrative will be limited to the events that are experienced by the narrator and will be told in the distinctive voice and language of that character.

Activity 4

Look at the two different versions of the same narrative below.

1 Identify which is a third-person narrative and which is a first-person narrative.

2 Note down the possible advantages and disadvantages of using each form of narrative.

Version A

I crashed the car when I heard. We were in the car park at the shopping centre. Faye said, "Jess, I'm getting married." She paused, no longer than a split second. "I'm getting married to Maxie." It was like being punched in the stomach. And as I was trying to catch my breath, the car slammed into the post with a sickening crunch. I hurtled into my seatbelt, then slumped back, winded again and speechless.

"What are you doing!" She screamed at me, "Are you crazy or something?"

I stared at her, but no words came. What could I say? Could I really tell her the truth?

Version B

Jess crashed the car when she heard. They were in the car park at the shopping centre. Faye said "Jess, I'm getting married." She paused, no longer than a split second. "I'm getting married to Maxie." Jess felt as if she had been punched in the stomach. As she was trying to catch her breath, the car slammed into the post with a sickening crunch. Jess hurtled into her seatbelt, then slumped back, winded and speechless.

Faye was terrified. "What are you doing!" She screamed at Jess. "Are you crazy or something?" She had thought that Jess would be happy for her, but it didn't seem that way. Jess just stared at her and said nothing.

Jess looked at Faye and wondered whether to tell her the truth.

You should certainly have decided before you go into your controlled assessment what point of view you are going to be writing from. If you have been asked to write a monologue, you already know it will be in the first person, but you may still have the choice of which character's point of view to use. Other kinds of narrative require you to make more fundamental choices. Before you do so, it may be helpful to weigh up the advantages and disadvantages of the different options.

Activity 5

Think about the narrative you have been creating in this lesson based on the stimulus in Activity 1.

1 Make a list of the possible points of view from which you could choose to narrate your story. Consider what different characters' perspectives you could use to write a first-person narrative.

2 Decide which of these you think will work best and write the first three paragraphs of your narrative, including the opening. Be prepared to explain why you have made the choices you have.

3 Descriptive writing

ResultsPlus
Build better answers

Look at this controlled assessment task:

Write a text titled 'Tomorrow'. Focus on descriptive writing.

■ A Band 3 answer will **have a clear sense of purpose** in which you **have well-chosen vocabulary and some evidence of crafting**. This might mean you select present tense verbs such as 'running' to make the writing sound exciting and positive.

● A Band 4 answer will be **a secure realisation of the task** with **aptly chosen vocabulary and variety**. This means you may begin to choose words to create a pattern through your writing – such as using 'jagged', 'cut' and 'strafe' if you want to suggest that the future will be violent.

▲ A Band 5 answer will be **strong** and **consistent**, with an extensive vocabulary. This means that you can choose the best word in each situation. This could be as complex as 'apocalyptic' or as simple as 'hope'.

If you are writing a description or a narrative for your controlled assessment task, your writing will need to include **descriptive writing**. To achieve the best marks you need to make your descriptions vivid and effective. First, you must think about the thing that you want to describe, such as the location where your piece is based, and the impressions you want to create.

Activity ①

Think about the setting suggested to you by the image on the right. Answer the following questions by brainstorming words and phrases:

1 What do you want your readers to know about this place?

2 What do you want them to feel about this place?

3 What language might you use in order to evoke these feelings in a reader?

Adjectives and **adverbs** are important tools in any description. As a writer you have to make choices about how many adjectives and adverbs you use, what kinds and how often. Beware of using too many – a few well-chosen ones work far better than saturating your writing with 'empty' and obvious description.

Activity ②

Read the two extracts on the opposite page. They illustrate two very different types of description.

1 For each extract, decide to what extent the writer has used:

   • impressionistic adjectives or adverbs (those which appeal to our senses and create a vivid, immediate impression)

   • factual adjectives or adverbs (those which simply supply us with information).

2 What impression of setting, character and mood do you get from each extract? Why might this be?

3 Rewrite one of the extracts, experimenting with different forms of description by removing, adding or substituting words. Explain what effect your changes have on the overall mood of the piece.

Text A

He slammed the car door and swore loudly. A pretty woman with two unnaturally neat-looking children in tow tutted at him as she passed. He caught her eye as she glanced at his battered old Mondeo. Certainly it had seen better days, and so had he, but there was no need to sneer. He watched her as she strode purposefully down the street and into one of the grander houses, her blonde ponytail swinging rhythmically. Blooming snobs, he thought.

Text B

I peer up at the sky, bright and blinding and oppressive. Everything is still – even the birds, who usually swoop and soar, are too hot to sing today. I roll over, the sticky grass leaving its indelible green signature on my trousers as I do so. I should get up. I glance over at Mary sleeping in the blue shade of a poplar tree and contemplate going back to the house, but the arrogant sun compels me to stay, lulling me back into half-sleep and stillness.

You can enrich your description by the occasional use of **similes** and **metaphors**, preferably your own original comparisons. Don't overdo it though – one or two may be all you need to enhance the vividness of the picture being drawn.

Activity 3   Look at the description of landscape below.

1 Rewrite this paragraph, following the suggestions for adding similes and metaphors.

1 Insert a simile to describe the sun here – 'like …'

2 Add a sentence comparing the sea to something, e.g. 'The sea was spread out like a …'.

3 Add adjectives that personify the harbour and the ships (present them as if they were people).

> The sun was shining 1...................... over the land and the sea. 2...................... In the distance the 3...................... harbour waited to welcome the 3...................... ships heading home. Sheep 4...................... were grazing on the slopes under the care of their shepherd as further up a ploughman carved furrows from the 5...................... soil.

4 Insert a metaphor to describe the sheep.

5 The verb 'carved' in this sentence is part of an extended metaphor to describe the nature of the soil; insert an adjective here that continues the same metaphor.

2 Now choose just one or two similes or metaphors that you think would be most effective in your own creative writing, and state your reasons.

4 Monologues

This lesson will help you to...

→ **create interesting and imaginative monologues**

A monologue is an extended speech by a character addressed to another character or to the audience. It can tell part or all of a story and gradually reveal the character's thoughts, feelings and attitudes. The story it tells can be simple, but it should reveal the truth about the narrator and the events they describe.

Activity 1   Read the monologue below.

I'd just taken her tea up this morning when she said, 'Graham, I think the world of you.' I said, 'I think the world of you.' And she said, 'That's all right then.' I said 'What's brought this on?' She said, 'Nothing. This tea looks strong, pull the curtains.' Of course I knew what had brought it on. She said, 'I wouldn't like you to think you're not Number One.' So I said, 'Well you're Number One with me too. Give me your teeth. I'll swill them.'

1   What does the monologue reveal about the character of the narrator and his relationship with his mother?

2   How is it different from a narrative you might find in a novel?

The first step in writing a monologue is to create your character and to make some key decisions about them.

Activity 2   Look at the two photographs to the left.

1   Copy and complete the profile below, using one of the two photographs as a stimulus to create the character for your monologue.

Name:	
Age:	**Gender:**
Where do they live?	
What is their occupation?	**What do they feel about this?**
What family do they have?	**How do they feel about them?**
Who is their closest friend?	
Think of five things they love	**Think of five things they hate**
Think of one thing they fear	**Think of one thing they dream about**
Optimist or pessimist?	

The story your monologue tells can begin in the middle – you can throw your readers straight in at the deep end.

Activity 3

Answer these key questions to help you develop the story of the character you created in Activity 2.

1 Imagine that something significant has just happened in the life of your character. What, exactly?

2 Imagine they face some sort of decision as a result of the significant event. What is it?

3 Imagine you are the character, talking directly to a friend about your thoughts and feelings on all of this. Write down what you would say, using the first person.

An individual's distinctive way of talking is called their **idiolect**. As a monologue is the voice of a character, when you write 'in their shoes' you also need to make some decisions about the way they speak.

Here are some techniques for creating a narrative voice in monologues:

- Use short or 'incomplete' sentences – write in the way that person would speak.
- Think about verb tense – using the present tense can make events seem very immediate.
- Think about the appropriate register and the kinds of vocabulary your character is most likely to use.
- How much is your character likely to use non-standard English, e.g. some slang or dialect?
- People often report dialogue when they speak, for example, 'He told me that the train was definitely going to be delayed'. You might want to do this in your monologue to help move on your narrative.

ResultsPlus

Controlled assessment tip

Before attempting to write a monologue or script, it might help to read the section on dialogue on pages 140–141 and complete some of the activities on spoken language from this book (especially pages 168–175).

Activity 4

Think about your character's idiolect.

1 Decide on the following:

a) How formal or colloquial is their vocabulary?

b) What are their favourite phrases and/or verbal mannerisms?

c) Are they usually serious, jokey, sarcastic, or emotional?

d) Do they tend to speak in long, rambling sentences, or use short, abrupt phrases?

e) Does their speech reflect their local accent or dialect?

2 Write roughly half a page of the monologue for your character, thinking about the decisions you made in Question 1.

5 Scripts

If you choose to write a script in response to your controlled assessment task, you need to write effective speech, as you would in a monologue. However, as scripts involve more than one person speaking, you will need to create a distinctive voice for each character and interesting dramatic dialogue. The words you put into the mouths of your characters should reveal their personalities and their relationships and develop an engaging story.

Activity ❶

Choose two of the characters shown in the images below.

1 For each character you have chosen, complete a copy of this profile:

Name:

Age:

Occupation:

Five things they like:

Five things they hate:

Where are they?

What has just happened?

What happens next?

How do they feel about what is happening?

2 Now decide how your two characters would speak. Write a short monologue for each one in which they introduce themselves. Think carefully about the following questions as you write the monologues:

- Do they speak formally or informally?
- What kinds of colloquial language, slang, or even technical jargon do they use as part of their idiolect?
- What kinds of sentences do they use?
- Are they serious or humorous?
- Are they confident or hesitant?

3 Next decide what the relationship is between your two characters and what situation you are going to put them in. Answer the questions below to help you make notes about the relationship.

   a) How do the characters know each other? What is their relationship?

   b) What are the characters' attitudes towards each other and why?

   c) Decide where, when, how and why they come to be speaking to each other.

   d) What does each character want to achieve from the conversation with the other? This is their motivation or objective.

   e) How, and why, does the conversation eventually come to an end?

When writing your script, you first need to set the scene. These instructions will be used by the stage or set designer when your script is performed. Here is an example of **scene-setting instructions**.

> *Ben, a middle-aged man in a clown's costume, is waiting at a bus stop with an old lady, Meg. Ben is carrying a newspaper, which he glances at from time to time. Meg is carrying a shopping bag and peers down the road looking for the bus, but cannot resist an occasional curious glance at Ben, to her right.*

Activity ②

Think about the dialogue and storyline you are going to create for the two characters in your script.

1 Write a short paragraph of instructions in which you set the scene for their dialogue, describing the setting, the characters' appearance and how they are positioned.

As you write your script, you should also include **stage directions**, which tell the actors how to play the parts of the characters and speak their lines. There are two kinds of stage direction:

*   Directions to the actor about how to speak a line, usually given before the actual words to be spoken.

*   Directions about actions to be performed by the actors or things that happen during the scene. These are often written in italics between lines of dialogue.

> **Ben:**   *(cheerfully)* Nice morning for it, isn't it?
> *There is a long, awkward pause as Meg stares at Ben's face and hair. The sounds of passing traffic are heard.*
> **Ben:**   I said, it's a nice morning, isn't it?

Activity ③

1 Write the script for the conversation between your two characters, which you have been planning during the lesson.

For more information on scripts, look at pages 168–171.

6 Creating characters

This lesson will help you to...

→ create interesting and realistic characters

Most creative writing tasks will require you to create at least one character. You will need to consider what your characters are like and how you can make them convincing people who have complex feelings, a history and reasons for saying and doing the things they do. In 1000 words you will only have time to create one or two realistic characters.

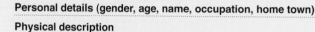

Activity 1

1. Start to create your own realistic character by looking at the photo on the left and by completing a copy of the profile below.

Personal details (gender, age, name, occupation, home town)
Physical description
What are this character's greatest hopes and wishes?
Do they tell other people about these?
What are this character's fears? Do they fear being lonely? Being poor? Do they have something to hide?
Is the character happy at the moment? Why or why not?
Personal relationships: who are the most important people in this character's life?
What are the character's strengths and weaknesses?
How would this character describe herself?
How would other people describe this character?
Language habits: does this character have an accent or dialect or other style of speech? Perhaps there are particular phrases she uses?

Now you need to decide how much of this information you want to reveal to your readers and how you are going to do this. Five of the main techniques that you can use to create a convincing character are shown below along with examples:

1 Physical description	He was an old man with a wizened face, drifts of fine white hair catching in the wind, a mischievous grin and a twinkle in the eye that spoke of many youthful adventures.
2 Description of character's thoughts, personality and feelings	He had always been a practical man given to action and invention rather than reflection. But now the torrents of grief for his lost son overwhelmed him. Wasn't he to blame?
3 Narration of the character's actions	At the memorial to his son, he stood motionless, his head bowed. He appeared not to hear the words spoken by the priest, his hands clutching an old, tatty book.
4 Quotation of the character's speech	"Oh, yes, very good," the old man enthused. "That will do nicely."
5 Creation of an 'inner monologue' of the character's thoughts	This was just fabulous. As the wind whistled through his hair and his tongue tasted the salt tang of the sea, he felt an extraordinary exhilaration. This was it. Life was finally beginning!

Activity 2

1 Imagine you are writing a narrative about the character you started to create in Activity 1. Write five paragraphs that reveal information about your character, using each of the five techniques listed opposite in turn.

Many writers advise that it is better just to show your character to the reader rather than telling them everything there is to know about them. In other words, leave your reader to draw their own conclusions.

Activity 3

Look at the following two pairs of character descriptions.

1 For each pair, decide which 'shows' and which 'tells' the reader about the character.

Version A

I was feeling extremely scared by the time we reached the dark cellar. I had never felt more nervous in my life.

Version B

By the time we reached the bottom of the cellar the hairs on the back of my neck were standing up, my flesh was prickling with goosebumps, and my pulse was racing.

Version A

My friend Michael shuffled and pretended to yawn, though I could tell he was scared too. "Hurry up then," he moaned. "I'm missing Coronation Street for this." But I noticed his eyes kept darting nervously to the door.

Version B

My friend Michael never liked anyone to know when he was scared – he always wanted to seem hard and in control. He kept making sarcastic remarks to try to convince me he wasn't really afraid.

ResultsPlus
Controlled assessment tip

Check your work for clichés and check that you haven't told your reader what to think. Be original and be suggestive and then you will be compelling.

2 Which type of description more effectively allows the reader to form their own impressions of the character? Why?

3 Write one further paragraph of the narrative about the character you have created in this lesson. Focus on how you might 'show' rather than 'tell' the reader about them.

7 Writing dialogue

This lesson will help you to...

→ **write using the voice of a character**

You can use dialogue to enrich and enliven your creative writing. When writing a narrative, the dialogue you include should reflect the personalities, emotions and thoughts of the characters you have created, just as it would if you were writing a script or a monologue. Dialogue can also communicate a lot about the relationships between your characters and how they view each other.

Activity 1

1 Match each of the pieces of dialogue below to the appropriate description of the characters.

2 For each example, write a short paragraph explaining the feelings and relationships between the characters and how the writer's use of dialogue helps to show these. For example, is the speech short and clipped, or long and drawn out? What type of vocabulary is used? Is there repeated or emphatic use of any particular personal pronouns such as 'I' or 'you'? What do these things tell us?

Dialogue

> "But you will be quiet now," said Father, raising his voice and interrupting him because none of the rules of normal family life ever applied to him. "I have been very considerate of your feelings here, Bruno, because I know that this move is difficult for you. And I have listened to what you have to say, even though your youth and inexperience force you to phrase things in an insolent manner. And you'll notice that I have not reacted to any of this. But the moment has come when you will simply have to accept that –"
> "I don't want to accept it!" shouted Bruno.
> "Go to your room, Bruno."

> 'I think we should head down.'
> 'I don't know...no, not down. We must keep in touch with the ridge. Didn't you see those flutings on this side? We'd never get back up again.'
> 'Have we got past that second summit?'
> 'I think so, yes.'
> 'I can't see anything up there.'

> Slim sat down on a box and George took his place opposite.
> 'It wasn't nothing,' said Slim. 'I would of had to drowned most of 'em, anyways. No need to thank me about that.'
> George said, 'It wasn't much to you, maybe, but it was a hell of a lot to him. Jesus Christ, I don't know how we're gonna get him to sleep in here. He'll want to sleep right out in the barn with 'em. We'll have trouble keepin' him from getting right in the box with them pups.'
> 'It wasn't nothing,' Slim repeated.

Description of characters

> Two agricultural labourers on a ranch in a western state of the USA.

> Two climbers trying to descend a large snowy mountain in very bad weather conditions.

> A parent and child talking about their recent change of home.

ResultsPlus
Controlled assessment tip

Identify two or three points in your controlled assessment task where you think dialogue could bring key moments to life, highlight key traits of your character or move the narrative on.

Selective use of dialogue can also help to progress your story and bring crucial episodes to life. Think of these as short pieces of drama which you can introduce into your narrative at key points. You could even try starting with a short burst of dialogue which plunges your readers straight into the action. You can also progress your narrative through using dialogue by making your characters talk about incidents that the reader might not have known about before. This is sometimes known as **exposition**.

Activity 2

1   Think back to the character you created in the previous lesson. Create a short section of dialogue between this character and another character. You might choose a topic which has been in a recent news story you have heard about. Try and make sure that your characters are reflected in the dialogue which you use.

You can read more about creating effective dialogue on pages 174 – 175.

Assessment practice

Here is an example of a controlled assessment style task you could be set. You will be expected to structure your story effectively.

Activity 3   Write a response to this question:

Write two paragraphs of a narrative in response to the title 'The Knock'. Focus on how well you structure the narrative.

You should spend 20 minutes on this task.

Look at this image.

Write a narrative entitled 'The Knock'. (24 marks)

ResultsPlus
Self assessment

Before you complete this self-assessment activity, you might like to read some sample answers to this task on the following pages (142-143).

1   **Check your answer to Activity 3:**
  • Have you developed an original and distinctive idea?
  • Have you considered how your opening links to the ending of your narrative?
  • Have you thought about how the structure of your writing will impact on the reader?

2   **Now decide which Band your answer to Activity 3 should fall into by applying the mark scheme opposite. You will need to be careful and precise in your marking.**

■ Band 3
  • ideas are developed appropriately
  • well-chosen vocabulary and some crafting of sentences
  • controlled use of paragraphs and successful use of cohesive devices

● Band 4
  • ideas are effective and sustained
  • aptly chosen vocabulary and variety in the construction of sentences
  • effective paragraphing and cohesive devices used within and between paragraphs

▲ Band 5
  • compelling and fully developed idea
  • extensive vocabulary
  • convincing organisation of ideas and sophisticated control of structure

Maximise your marks

Write two paragraphs of a narrative entitled 'The Knock'. You should focus on how well you structure your narrative.

Here are three student answers to the narrative task on page 141. Read the answers together with the examiner comments around and after the answers. Then complete the activity at the bottom of page 143.

A strong opening that gives the sense of an ending to the story.

An effectively developed paragraph, especially the short sentences for the knock that sound sudden.

> Opening the door was a mistake. He knew that now.
> Settling in front of the TV, Danny kicked off his shoes and warmed his feet by the fire. It was a dismal day outside and so was a perfect chance to settle down on his new leather sofa and watch football on the plasma. A knock. It wasn't the time or the type of day to expect visitors. He waited a while. Should he go? His feet were warmed through and there was a chance of a goal. Another knock. Urgent. Insistent. Danny moved slowly to his door. Tugging it open he peered into the gap he created.

This is a clever use of short sentences that help to build suspense in the writing.

Examiner summary

This part of the answer is typical of a grade B performance. Student 1 has effectively hooked the reader with the opening sentence and has given a sense of structure by hinting at an event that happens later in the story. The setting and the knocking are developed appropriately and this is sustained throughout the paragraph.

The use of 'he' and 'she' is a clever device for retaining mystery and emphasising the gender divide, and keeps us engaged in the text.

> She knocked, knocked hard. He would answer — both the door and the million questions that she had stored, ready to interrogate him. She didn't normally knock; she normally would walk in as if this was her home. He destroyed the security offered by a home and now she must wait to be invited in.
> She knew he would be pausing the football and loping in annoyance to the door. He would be questioning who didn't know him well enough to come calling on a Saturday afternoon. He would be searching for the key and wishing people knew to walk around to the side door. She knew she should use the side door but she didn't want to accept that she knew him at all.

A development of the idea using appropriate examples to support the point made.

Examiner summary

This part of the answer is typical of a grade A performance. The idea is original as the use of 'he' and 'she' puts the reader in an interesting position, as they are trying to work out who they should blame for the situation. The structure is clearly organised around the chronological events of the woman's visit to the man's house.

This is an interesting beginning that hooks the reader.

A clear indication of structure, persuading the reader that text will develop logically.

It started with a tapping. It wasn't until it was too late that it was a knocking. John knew he should have moved but, well, the bed was too comfortable. It wasn't his fault.

Let me start at the beginning, dear reader. As your story-teller I must inform you that I was present in the attic and in the bedroom and well, wherever else I choose to lead you. The tapping started in the attic, just above where John slept. A small inhuman creature, restless, requested attention. It tapped for hours, patient in his task at first. It wriggled its sore legs a little in frustration at times but kept to a rhythmic tap.

The narrator unusually addresses the reader directly and this will make the writing stand out amongst others.

Examiner summary

This part of the answer is typical of a grade A* performance. The student has selected an unusual idea and the narrative perspective is also distinct. The structure is indicated in the opening paragraph and at the beginning of the second paragraph – the reader trusts that the writer knows how they are going to progress the narrative.

Results**Plus**
Build better answers

Move from a Grade Ⓑ to a Grade Ⓐ

In this part of the answer you need to begin to choose an idea that is different from the ones other people will choose to write. This will make your writing a little more engaging. Student 1 does have a fairly effective structure though it is not obvious where it is going next. Student 2 clearly shows they will be recounting the events chronologically.

Aim for a Grade Ⓐ*

In this part of the answer you need to come up with a clear structure and voice. Student 3 chooses a second-person narrator and begins at the end. This immediately engages the reader and suggests unusual events have occurred. The writer has made choices about the structure and narrator with the effect they hope to achieve in mind.

Putting it into practice

1 Using the title 'The Stranger' think of unusual approaches to the piece of narrative writing.

2 Explore with a partner how your approach would be different if you chose to write a script instead.

8 Crafting vocabulary

Choosing the most effective vocabulary can transform a competent piece of writing into an excellent one. Sometimes writers choose words not just for their meanings, but also for the combination of sounds or a particular mood or feeling. Don't forget though that the vocabulary you choose must be appropriate to the context of your writing.

One of the key ways of creating particular sounds and moods with words is the use of devices such as **alliteration** (repetition of the initial sounds in words, e.g. 'the dull, dreary day'), **assonance** (repetition of vowel sounds in words next to or near each other, e.g. 'his brief was to sweep the street clean') and **onomatopoeia** (use of words which sound like what they describe, e.g. 'screech').

Activity ①

The writer of the passage below wished to create a soundscape, contrasting the impressions of a lively, noisy street and the eerie silence of the underground cellar below.

1 and 2 hum/roar/murmur/din

3 splutter/rumble/clatter/outburst

4 howl/gasp/wail/sigh

5 screeched/ground/came/shuddered

6 closed/slammed/eased

7 called/shouted/yelled/bawled

8 calling/wailing/screeching/ululation

9 sigh/whisper/gasp/breath

10 sounds/footstep/footfall

11 rubbing/susurration/rustling

At street level, the 1..................... and 2..................... of traffic was punctuated by the occasional 3..................... of human activity and the 4..................... of the gusty wind. Delivery vans 5..................... to a halt; doors were 6..................... shut, workmen 7..................... and the 8..................... of a siren sliced through the noise of the day.

Only a few feet below, in the underground cellar, there was barely a 9..................... of wind. In the perfect silence there was only our own feathered 10....................., the 11..................... of silk and cotton, the gentle 12..................... of our breathing and the occasional 13..................... of a nervous cough. Somewhere we heard a door 14..................... and the 15..................... of running water.

1 Select the word you think would be most effective to fill each of the numbered gaps, choosing from the options given. For the last four you will need to suggest your own. Look up words in a dictionary if you need to.

2 Write down the reason for each of your choices of word – what sound, mood or feeling does it create in the text and how?

When you narrate actions and events, it is important to think carefully about your choice of **verbs**. For example, if you describe someone walking down the street, do you write that they merely walked – or strolled, sauntered, skipped, waddled, rushed, marched, ambled or prowled? Choosing the verb with precisely the right **connotations** (ideas that are implied or suggested by a word) can help your readers visualise more clearly the actions you are describing.

Activity 2

Look at the simple verbs in the box below.

1 Suggest three alternatives that could be used in place of each verb. Explain the different connotations of each alternative. An example is provided for each one to get you started.

run: *sprint, …*	eat: *nibble, …*	shake: *tremble, …*
speak: *whisper, …*	wait for: *anticipate, …*	give: *offer, …*
hold: *grab, …*	fall: *stumble, …*	stop: *terminate, …*
kill: *slaughter, …*	save: *rescue, …*	think: *reflect, …*

Results Plus
Controlled assessment tip

Think about some of the verbs you might need to use to report and describe actions and events in your controlled assessment task. Challenge yourself to think of alternatives to the simpler, more obvious words you might think of first.

Most narratives are written in the **past tense**, but there are exceptions. Sometimes, a writer may choose to use the **present tense** for part or even all of a narrative in order to make it seem as if the events being described are really happening as we read.

Activity 3

1 Read the two versions below of the same episode from a narrative. Note the possible advantages and disadvantages of each method of reporting events.

Past-tense narration

Looking behind me, I turned the corner and started down the hill. Nobody was following, but I still had to try hard not to run. Keep calm, I told myself, keep focused. I just needed to get to Jen and explain what had happened before anyone else did. I passed a young couple, arms entangled, oblivious and carefree and I felt a sharp pang of jealousy. And then out of nowhere there he was, right in front of me, all my worst fears in a three-piece suit. "We need to talk," he said.

Present-tense narration

Looking behind me, I turn the corner and start down the hill. Nobody is following, but I still have to try hard not to run. Keep calm, I tell myself, keep focused. I just need to get to Jen and explain what happened before anyone else does. I pass a young couple, arms entangled, oblivious and carefree and I feel a sharp pang of jealousy. And then out of nowhere there he is, right in front of me, all my worst fears in a three-piece suit. "We need to talk," he says.

Results Plus
Watch out!

The 'usual' approach to narrative writing is to stick to past tense throughout. If you do decide to use present-tense narration, be absolutely clear exactly when you intend to do so and for what effect – and check your writing carefully to ensure you haven't been switching randomly between past and present tenses.

2 Write a paragraph in which you describe a particularly frightening experience in your life. Think about the adjectives, verbs and adverbs you will use and try to employ some devices such as onomatopoeia to evoke atmosphere and the emotion of the character(s) involved. Will you use present or past-tense narration? Why?

9 Crafting sentences

This lesson will help you to...

→ make creative and effective choices of sentence length and construction

You can create subtle effects by constructing your sentences in different ways. Changing the way a sentence is built can subtly alter the meaning and create a different effect on the reader. It is often most effective to alter your use of **verbs** and **adverbs**.

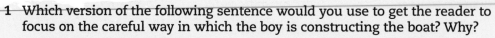

Activity 1

1 Which version of the following sentence would you use to get the reader to focus on the careful way in which the boy is constructing the boat? Why?

A **Slowly and deliberately**, Jack attached each sail to the model boat.

B Jack attached each sail **slowly and deliberately** to the model boat.

C Jack attached each sail to the model boat **slowly and deliberately**.

2 Which version of the following sentence would you use to give the reader the strongest possible impression of speed? Why?

A The two birds soon gained height, **soaring rapidly** above the waves and **accelerating** skywards with each beat of their wings.

B **Soaring rapidly** above the waves, the two birds soon gained height, each beat of their wings **accelerating** them skywards.

C **Rapidly soaring** above the waves, **accelerating** skywards with each beat of their wings, the two birds soon gained height.

Another set of choices you have as a writer is between **active** and **passive** sentences. Look at this example:

Jack slowly and deliberately attached each sail to the model boat **(active)**

Each sail was attached slowly and deliberately to the model boat by Jack **(passive)**

In general, writers often prefer active sentences for clarity and simplicity, but passive sentences can be useful; for example, you can choose whether or not to include the person or thing responsible for the action – here, 'by Jack'.

Activity 2

Look at this series of sentences from a narrative about a runaway boy and consider the different effects that could be created by using active or passive sentences.

1 Which version of the following sentence would you use to stress that when the boy tiptoed out of the house, nobody took much notice? Why?

A No one observed the boy climbing out of the window **(active)**.

B The boy climbed out of the window unobserved **(active)**.

C The boy climbing out of the window was observed by no one **(passive)**.

2 Which version of the following sentence would you use to focus on the foolish behaviour of the boy? Why?

A The boy either ignored, or did not hear, the desperate appeals of his parents (**active**).

B The desperate appeals of his parents were either ignored, or unheard (**passive**).

C The desperate appeals of his parents were either ignored or unheard by the boy (**passive**).

3 Which version of the following sentence would you use to stress that the circumstances of the boy's disappearance were widely accepted as true?

A Many people said that the boy ran away with a friend from school (**active**).

B The boy was said to have run away with a friend from school (**passive**).

Assessment practice

Here is an example of a controlled assessment task you could be set. You will be expected to use appropriate and effective language.

Activity 3

Write a response to this question:

Write the final paragraph of a narrative entitled 'The Knock'. You should focus on how well you craft the language that you use.

You should spend 10 minutes on this task.

Look at this image.

Write a narrative entitled 'The Knock'. (24 marks)

ResultsPlus
Self assessment

Before you complete this self-assessment activity, you might like to read some sample answers to this task on the following pages (148-149).

1 **Check your answer to Activity 3:**
  • Have you developed an original and distinctive idea?
  • Have you selected language that is meant to have an impact on the reader?
  • Have you selected language that represents the ideas that you wished to explore?

2 **Now decide which Band your answer to Activity 3 should fall into by applying the mark scheme opposite. You will need to be careful and precise in your marking.**

Band 3
  • ideas are expressed clearly
  • well-chosen vocabulary
  • punctuation is mostly selected for emphasis and effect
  • sentences are clearly structured, with control over how they sound

Band 4
  • ideas are effective throughout
  • aptly chosen vocabulary
  • variety in the construction of sentences
  • precise use of punctuation for effect

Band 5
  • compelling and fully developed ideas
  • an extensive vocabulary
  • convincing sentences
  • sophisticated use of punctuation

Maximise your marks

Write the final paragraph of a narrative entitled 'The Knock'.

You should focus on how well you craft the language that you use.

Here are three student answers to the task on page 147. Read the answers together with the examiner comments around and after the answers. Then complete the activity at the bottom of page 149.

Here are three student answers to the task on page 147. Read the answers together with the examiner comments around and after the answers. Then complete the activity at the bottom of page 149.

Student 1 – Extract typical of a grade (B) answer

Good verb choices used throughout.

Clever use of questions to give the effect of confusion.

> A simple choice to tug open a door had changed so much. If Danny had stayed slouched on the settee, warming his feet, all would be well. Laid out on his floor was this stranger, a gash deep in his forehead. The crowd cheered. Another goal? Another victory for his team? Danny felt as if they were jeering him — mocking him — for a victorious fight that would bring his life to a close.

The dashes help build up pace in the writing and show how much the cheering is upsetting him.

Examiner summary

This part of the answer is typical of a grade B performance. The punctuation and verb choices are particularly effective in this closing paragraph and these choices are made throughout the extract. The idea is effectively developed through the choice to use questions and the pattern of three to highlight the character's upset and confusion.

Student 2 – Extract typical of a grade (A) answer

This simple sentence is effective as it mimics the pause that it describes.

> He cried and reached out for her hand. A gentle brush of a finger. She dragged her hand away. She couldn't persuade her eyes to move from his. They paused. Without cue she slipped beside him and coaxed him to her. He laid his head on her chest like a small boy and heaved into his tears.

Continuous choice of strong verbs shows that language choices are sustained.

Examiner summary

This part of the answer is typical of a grade A performance. Top grade performance does not have to be elaborate. It can be powerful in its simplicity. The end of this section engages the reader through the use of emotion. The simple and sometimes purposely incomplete sentences mimic the hesitant movements of the couple. These choices are clearly crafted.

A clever use of questions directed at the reader.

A deceptively mysterious ending which has a nice rhythm to it, aimed at leaving the reader a little unnerved.

You ask me for a moral, dear reader. How strange that you want meaning from all events. A small alien child was living in a man's attic. A runaway. The warning taps went unheeded and the man was crushed amongst the debris caused by the rampant mother alien who came knocking. Really, what moral could there be? Check your attic for small alien creatures? Don't ignore tapping? Make sure you exit your house before large green aliens rampage over your bed? Let's just leave the events as a tragic accident of imagination and smile smugly in bed when the tapping starts above your head.

Clever use of an ironic voice.

Examiner summary

This part of the answer is typical of a grade A* performance. The crafting of the ironic tone of voice through the use of 'dear reader' and the use of questions sets this final paragraph apart. An original idea and clever ending when referring to the reader who might also ignore tapping.

ResultsPlus
Build better answers

**Move from a Grade to a Grade **

In this part of the answer you need to realise that choices do not need to be elaborate but just effective. Student 1 made effective choices but did not sustain this through the piece. Student 2 made simple but effective choices throughout.

**Aim for a Grade **

In this part of the answer you need to create a distinctive voice through the use of words and sentence choice. Student 2's answer lacked a strong voice that would engage the reader. Student 3 cleverly used a second person narrator and an ironic tone through the use of humour and rhetorical questions.

Putting it into practice

1   Try writing three different versions of the opening of a narrative called 'Holiday'. Try to capture a different voice each time.

Controlled assessment practice

Guidance for students: Creative Writing Task

What do I have to do?
You will complete one task on creative writing, from a choice of four.
You must complete this task on your own.

How much time do I have?
Following preparation, you will have up to two hours to complete this task.

How do I prepare for the task?
Choose the task.

Review the stimulus material provided for the task with your teacher. Stimulus materials will be based on themes which are shared with the Edexcel Poetry Anthology themes; **however,** it is not necessary to study the poems for the writing task. Any theme may be chosen.

You will be given guidance about creative writing, which may include:
- the content - real or imagined events
- your audience
- the 'voice' you may want to use
- any plot or narrative structure
- the structural features of your writing
- creation of character and use of dialogue
- creation of setting and atmosphere
- appropriate language techniques
- use of imagery
- use of rhetorical devices.

You should then prepare by making notes and planning your response to the task.

What must my response to the task show?
The response must show that you can:
- write clearly, effectively, and imaginatively in your chosen form to engage the reader
- make sure your spelling, punctuation and grammatical structures are accurate and appropriate for purpose and effect.

How should I present my response?
A written response of up to 1000 words.

The Creative Writing Task for the student

Choose one theme and complete the task from the choice below.

The text may be one of the following:
- Narrative
- Description
- Monologue
- Script

Examiner's tip

Answer one task below using one of these forms.

Theme A: Relationships
Task: Look at the image on the website. Write a text which explores EITHER the events leading up to this moment OR the events which directly follow this moment   (24)

Robert Doisneau, *Le Baiser de l'Hôtel de Ville* (1950)

Theme B: Clashes and Collisions
Task: Look at the video clip. Write a text from the viewpoint of a person in this video clip.   (24)

Euronews G20 London protests

Theme C: Somewhere, Anywhere
Task: Look at the image. Write a text titled 'A place of my own'.   (24)

'For Sale' house sign

Theme D: Taking a Stand
Task: Listen to the podcast on the website. Write a text based on the activities of a campaigner.   (24)

Japan's whaling fleets in the Antarctic halted its operations today while they decide what to do with two anti-whaling activists who've been detained by the crew of a Japanese harpoon ship that they climbed on board. This is the moment it happened…

Guardian podcast — Paul Watson (3 min 59)

All the sample controlled assessment stimulus material is available at www.edexcel.com.

Unit 3 Spoken Language

This unit is a GCSE English Language unit. If you are taking GCSE English, turn to page 124 for Unit 3 Creative English: Writing.

The Spoken Language unit gives you the opportunity to develop your speaking and listening skills, complete a spoken language study and produce a piece of writing for the spoken voice. This student book unit focuses on the spoken language study and spoken voice tasks.

Spoken Language is all around us. In this unit you will explore both scripted speech, for example in TV scripts and plays, and spontaneous speech, which could be your own everyday language, the language of people your age, the language you hear around you or that you hear on TV, radio and the internet.

This section of the book will help you to identify features of spoken language, both scripted and spontaneous, and to understand the effects that it has on different audiences. You will also investigate the different reasons why people choose to use language differently in certain situations. The texts and activities you will encounter as you develop these skills are all focused on helping you to achieve the best grade you can in your controlled assessment tasks.

Your assessment

This unit is a controlled assessment unit for GCSE English Language. You will complete **two** writing tasks: a Spoken Language Study and Writing for the Spoken Voice.

In the **Spoken Language Study** section, you will complete **one** task from a choice of **two** in which you will be asked to explore the way spoken language works. You will have up to two hours to complete this task and you can write up to 1000 words. You will be given the task in advance so that you have time to plan your response so that you feel prepared to complete this part of the controlled assessment.

In your response to the spoken language task, you will need to:

✔ show how spoken language changes depending on the context

✔ show understanding of some of the choices people make when they are speaking.

In the **Writing for the Spoken Voice** section, you will complete **one** task from a choice of **three** and write either a speech, a story with lots of direct speech, or a script for a specific media type, such as a radio drama or TV soap. You will either be given a word limit of 1000 words or a limit of the equivalent of between 30 seconds and 2 minutes of spoken language. You will be given the task in advance so that you have time to plan your response so that you feel prepared to complete this part of the controlled assessment.

Your response to the writing for the spoken voice task must show that you:

✔ understand that different media work in different ways

✔ understand the needs of different audiences and purposes.

Assessment Objectives

Your response to the controlled assessment writing tasks of Unit 3 will be marked using these Assessment Objectives:

Spoken Language Study Task

✔ Understand variations in spoken language, explaining why language changes in relation to contexts.

✔ Evaluate the impact of spoken language choices in your own and others' use.

Writing for the Spoken Voice Task

✔ Write to communicate clearly, effectively and imaginatively, using and adapting forms and selecting vocabulary appropriate to task and purpose in ways that engage the reader.

✔ Organise information and ideas into structured and sequenced sentences, paragraphs and whole texts, using a variety of linguistic and structural features to support cohesion and overall coherence.

This student book unit will help you to understand what these require you to do so that you can write a successful response to your controlled assessment writing tasks.

1 Recognising spoken language

This lesson will help you to...
→ recognise the difference between written and spoken language
→ differentiate between spontaneous speech that has been transcribed and planned, scripted speech

We all use spoken language every day, so we are very familiar with it, but we tend to take it for granted. Spoken language is very different from written language. Each is used in different contexts.

Activity 1

Look at this box showing different contexts in which language is used:

job interview	poem	note	job application
class presentation	text message to a friend	coffee with a friend	soap opera on TV

1 Divide these language contexts into two lists under the headings in the table below. The first one has been done for you.

Spoken language	Written language
job interview	

Spoken language can be more **informal** or more **formal**, and more **planned (scripted)** or more **spontaneous**.

Activity 2

Look at all the examples of spoken language you identified in Activity 1.

1 Plot each example onto the chart below to show whether you would expect it to be more formal or more informal, and scripted or spontaneous.

Scripted

Informal ←——————→ Formal

Spontaneous

You need to be able to differentiate between spontaneous spoken language and planned scripted spoken language (that is, language that is written to be spoken aloud).

Activity ③

Read the two texts below (Texts A and B). One is a transcript of spontaneous spoken language – a written record of everything each speaker said. The other is an example of scripted language – planned speech for inclusion in a play, a television programme, a film, or a formal address.

1   Which is the transcript of spontaneous spoken language and which is the example of scripted spoken language?

2   What factors in each text made you reach this decision? Think about which is easier to understand, and which includes more repetition.

Text A

G: I think I've done all mine
A: Do they live in the water
G: I wonder where that one Karen Karen what is that
TA: It's a moorhen It's in that book
J: No
G: No that's a duck
A: And that's a swan

Text B

CLIENT:	I have a query regarding my account and I'd like to see the manager.
BANK CLERK:	Do you have your account details with you?
CLIENT:	Yes. Here they are.
BANK CLERK:	What is the problem, sir?

Activity ④

Listen to an example of a conversation in a TV drama such as the one provided on the ActiveTeach. This is scripted speech. Now listen to an example of people talking on a reality TV show. Again, an example is provided on the ActiveTeach. This is spontaneous spoken language. You might want to listen to these examples more than once.

1   Which is easier to understand – the drama or the reality show?

2   Did you observe any pauses or repetitions? Where did these occur?

3   In which one did people talk at the same time or interrupt each other most?

2 The features of spoken language

This lesson will help you to...

→ identify some of the features and structures of spoken language

→ understand why these occur

We don't plan most of the spoken language we use. Even in relatively formal situations, we don't plan our words before we speak. Spoken language will change depending on context and will respond to changes in that context, including the contribution of other speakers or the responses of others to what we say. This means that spoken language has a range of features that written language does not have. The following are some of the features of spoken language.

- **Pauses, repetition** and **fillers** – When people are talking, they will often hesitate, repeat what they have said and use fillers such as 'er' and 'erm' or 'you know'. This may be because the speaker is thinking about what to say, or it may carry a message to the listener. For example, do you think B is going to accept an invitation below or not?

  > A: D'you want to come round tonight?
  > B: (.) Er (.)

- **Incomplete structures** and **ellipsis** (leaving words out) – The meaning of spoken language can often be understood from the context, or from the knowledge that the speakers have about each other and the world. Full explanation when speaking is therefore unnecessary. For example:

  > Interviewer: So how did you feel?
  > Man: Gutted.

- **Deixis** (words and phrases specific to the context) – These are words that refer to the situation in which the speakers are operating, and cannot really be understood outside that context. They are words such as 'this', 'that', 'these', 'there', 'now', 'then', for example:

  > A: Excuse me. I'm looking for the station.
  > B: Just round that corner over there.

- **Hedges** – Phrases which make a statement less certain, for example, 'I believe that', 'it seems that', 'perhaps'. People sometimes think it is rude to make definite statements, particularly if they are correcting someone.

- **Taking turns, interruptions** and **overlaps** – In conversations, people take turns to speak and it is unusual to find gaps between turns. People may interrupt each other or talk at the same time as one speaker takes his or her turn before the previous speaker has finished.

- **Discourse markers** – Spoken language doesn't use punctuation. Boundaries between units of language or different topics can be marked by short pauses and words or phrases like 'okay', 'right', 'I mean'. These are called discourse markers.

- **Cooperation, back-channel** and **feedback** – When we are talking to each other, we cooperate. We speak, we listen and we give indications to show that we are listening and that we are aware of people listening to us. We say things like 'mm' and 'yeah' when someone else is speaking. This is called back-channelling or feedback, and we use tag questions like 'isn't it?' and 'you know?'. English has a very wide range of tag questions, but recently all-purpose tags like 'innit' and 'nahmean' have appeared, particularly among young people.

When spoken language is transcribed, the features of spoken language have to be included. This is done in the following ways:

Spoken language feature	How it is transcribed
Brief pause	(.)
Longer pause (including time in seconds)	(0.5)
People speaking at the same time	// words spoken at the same time as others //

Below is a transcript of children working with their teaching assistant. The transcript not only contains the words that the speakers used, but also shows features like pauses, interruptions and overlaps. Very little punctuation is used in transcripts.

G: I think I've done all mine

A: Do they live in the water

G: I wonder where that one (.) Karen (.) Karen what is that

TA: It's a moorhen (0.5) It's in that book

J: No

G: No that's a duck

A: And that's a swan

A: 's // not //

G: // What // is?

J: That

G: That might be a cygnet (3.0) might be a cygnet (.) might be a cygnet

Activity ❶   Read the transcript above. You can also listen to this sample of spoken language on the ActiveTeach.

1 Identify:

   a) a pause

   b) a place where two people are speaking at once

   c) an example of a context-bound word or phrase (deixis)

   d) an incomplete structure

   e) repetition.

2 Record your own example of spoken language, perhaps a conversation between two friends, and write a transcript of it, thinking about where there are pauses, repetitions and overlaps and why this might be.

3 Understanding contexts 1

→ explore the ways spoken language changes depending on the context

The way a person speaks is influenced by the context:

- **The topic** (sometimes called **field**) – what a speaker is talking about may affect the way he or she speaks.

- **Who is speaking, and to whom they are speaking** (sometimes called **tenor**) – a speaker's language may be influenced by where they come from and where they live. It may be affected by the cultural group they belong to, their age and their gender. It may also be influenced by the person they are speaking to and this person's age, gender and status.

- **Why they are speaking** (sometimes called **purpose**) – the reason why someone is speaking will also affect his or her language.

- **What kind of spoken language it is** (sometimes called **mode**) – it may be a chat, a phone call, an interview, a presentation, or a speech, for example.

Activity ❶

Read the transcripts below. Text A is an extract from an interview with a hip hop artist called Part 2 to publicise a new album. Text B is an interview with a woman who was born in 1924 about her life in a convent boarding school.

Text A

| Interviewer: | You've been around putting out vinyl since around 94 yeah? (.) I was wondering why it took so long from 97 when you released the Electronic Bombardment 12" and like it took two years later since Eye of the Hurricane came out? |
| Part 2: | It costs a lot of money nahmean n the first 12s we done ourselves (.) and after we signed to Big Dada* at that time they weren't really doing albums n that cos they had to set up the label n were only doing 12s to build up the label |

*a record label

Text B

| Interviewer: | What do you remember about your school days |
| Joan: | I was perfectly happy at school (.) not homesick and we had good fun and I enjoyed the company (0.5) It was weird when I first started but I soon got the hang of it (0.5) Early on (.) I got caught reading a comic (.) *Girl Friend* (.) before Mass (0.5) it was confiscated and the comic was no longer sent (0.5) I hadn't known the rules (0.5) it wasn't done to read a thing like that before Mass (.) it was a crime against God (0.5) Now (.) the religion we get rammed down our throats a bit but you assumed that was just part of being in a convent school (0.5) We had R.I. every day (.) went to mass each morning and benediction each afternoon |

1 Can you identify any examples of words or phrases that are influenced by the topic of each transcript?

2 What is the relationship between the interviewer and the interviewee (the tenor)? Does it affect the way they speak and the language they use?

3 What is the purpose of each interview? Who is the audience likely to be? How might this affect the language used?

Spoken language is influenced by where someone was born and lives. Each area of the UK has its own distinctive variety of English, including different grammatical forms and vocabulary. These forms are called **dialects**.

Accent is the way that spoken language is pronounced. There are many different accents, such as a Liverpool accent or a Birmingham accent.

Accent is not only associated with geographical region but also with particular groups: for example, many younger people now use 'upspeak', which features a rising tone once used only for questions. Received Pronunciation (RP) is the accent associated with the royal family and used in the past by broadcasters. The Mayor of London, Boris Johnson, is a good example of an RP speaker.

Standard English is a dialect which is not associated with any particular region or place. It can be spoken with any accent. When you write, you are expected to use complete sentences and to follow the rules of standard English – it is often seen as the 'correct' form of English. However, when people speak they often used non-standard forms which do not follow the rules of standard English.

For example:

- non-standard vocabulary – 'Hey' to mean 'Hello'
- non-standard grammar – 'I've not got none'

Activity ❷   Re-read Texts A and B on page 158.

1 Which interviewee uses standard English and which one uses a non-standard dialect?

2 Make a list of all the vocabulary and grammatical forms used by the interviewee who uses a non-standard dialect that are not found in standard English.

3 For each example you find, write a sentence explaining why it is used. Think about the four key points at the top of page 158.

ResultsPlus
Build better answers

Look at this part of a controlled assessment task:

Using two examples of spoken language, comment on the way teenagers adapt their spoken language to suit the situation. Comment on how the purpose of the spoken language affects the way it is used.

■ A Band 3 answer shows **clear understanding** of the ways in which spoken language changes according to context and why these changes occur. For example: *Like most people, teenagers change their language depending on who they are talking to and why. They will speak casually to their parents, but they won't use the same language they use when they are with their friends.*

● A Band 4 answer shows **assured understanding** of the ways spoken language changes according to context and why these changes occur. For example: *Teenagers adapt their language depending on the group they are with and the situation they are in. Their language will be very different when they are with their friends, when they are with other teenagers they don't know well, when they are talking to their teachers or other adults.*

▲ A Band 5 answer shows **perceptive understanding** of the ways in which spoken language works, the ways in which it changes according to context and why these changes occur. For example: *Teenagers have a range of language styles from formal through to informal, and in this respect, their language is no different from other adults. However, their attitudes to particular situations may vary, for example, non-standard forms, especially current slang, are often used by teenagers and they may be make sure they are using the appropriate non-standard form for the group they are with.*

Understanding contexts 2

In this lesson you will look at how **age**, **regional identity** and **gender** affect spoken language.

Let's look at the **age** of the speakers first. Read the transcript below. Beth, aged four, and Sammy, aged ten, are playing.

> Beth: Hello I on a phone
> Sammy: You're on the phone are you Bethany? // Hello //
> Beth: // Yes // (.) Hello
> Sammy: Hello Bethany
> Beth: er I on a phone
> Sammy: You're on the phone well // this //
> Beth: // yeah //
> Sammy: Well this this is my phone

Beth, at four years old, is still acquiring language and some of the structures she uses are incomplete. Sammy, her older sister, does what older people often do when they are talking to children: she doesn't correct Beth but she repeats what Beth has said, expanding it to give the complete form. Beth doesn't yet understand the difference between 'a' and 'the' and, again, Sammy models the correct form to her.

When adults talk to young children, they tend to use simpler sentence constructions, fewer ellipses (when words are left out) and a limited vocabulary.

Activity ❶

Read the transcript below. It records a conversation between four-year-old Beth and her grandmother. Beth is playing on the computer, pretending to work.

> G: Do you need this one? ─────────── If she was talking to an adult, Beth's grandmother would probably use ellipsis and just say 'This one?'.
> B: No I need (.) writing one
> G: You need the writing one OK
> B: Yeh I need writing cos writing is er my work
> G: OK well this is the writing one darling
> B: Yes I I writing
> G: You're writing are you?
>   (Beth types)

1 Find examples of:

a) child language

b) Beth's grandmother repeating and expanding on what Beth says

c) Beth's grandmother using a complete structure where she might have used ellipsis if she was talking to an adult. One example has been identified for you.

People's **regional identity** will affect the dialect and accent they have.
An individual's distinctive way of speaking is called their **idiolect**.

Activity ❷

Read the transcript below. A Sheffield man is talking about buying building materials.

1 Make a list of ways in which language is influenced by the speaker's regional identity – for example, any dialect words or grammatical forms used as well as any accent suggested. Some examples have been labelled to start you off.

George uses a verb form that is found in regional dialects in the north of England, the historic present. Standard English would use 'go' or 'went' here.

George: Anyway (.) I (.) I goes down there for some plaster (.) 20 kilo bags (.) I thought 20 kilo bags no prices anywhere in B and Q (.) so I just gets two bags like I were (.) I thought well there's nowhere in bloomin here for me to weigh these like so I takes a couple goes to counter (.) plaster board I gets so many plaster aboard an all (.) gets to counter (.) three eighty three three eighty for a little twenty kilo bag that's nowt

Gordon: Not behind door, B and Q

Dialect phrase meaning 'not stupid'

Sharing accent and dialect makes people feel like part of a cultural group and gives them a sense of belonging. However, some people might associate the use of regional accent and dialect with lower social status. People sometimes change their use of spoken language in order to avoid this, depending on the context.

Activity ❸

Think about a time you have changed the way you speak to fit the context. This may well have been because of the **mode** of spoken language required – for example, a phone call or an interview.

1 Write a paragraph describing the ways in which you changed your language – vocabulary, grammatical forms and accent – and explain why this was. What effect might these changes have had?

Finally, the **gender** of the speaker also affects the language used. Do men and women use language differently? There are a lot of stereotypes relating to language and gender. One is that males speak more than females, interrupt more and are more likely to introduce new topics. Females are supposed to be more polite and more likely to give support to other participants in conversations.

Activity ❹

Observe the way language is used around you. Listen to several of your friends talking.

1 Do the males and females act in the ways described above?

2 Does their behaviour change in different contexts?

3 Are males or females more likely to make contributions in class discussions?

5 Understanding language choices

This lesson will help you to...

→ appreciate the different levels of formality used for different contexts

→ understand how language choice is influenced by speaker relationship and purpose

Register means the form of language that is appropriate to a particular situation and context. For example, some situations are formal and require more formal language; others are more informal and language can be less formal. When people are talking in an **informal register**, they use casual terms of address (for example, 'mate', 'love' and first names), slang, more short forms and ellipsis. When they are talking in a **formal register**, they use more formal terms of address (title and family name, for example, 'Mrs Smith,' 'sir', 'madam'), less slang, fewer short forms and fewer examples of ellipsis.

It is important not to confuse regional dialects with informality. Some speakers always use regional dialect forms, but they will switch from an informal register to a more formal register at various points.

ResultsPlus
Controlled assessment tip

Don't confuse 'informal' with 'inappropriate'. Informal is often the appropriate choice for a particular context.

Activity ❶

Read the two transcripts of conversations that follow. Text A is a fairground stallholder talking to customers; you can listen to the audio recording of this on the ActiveTeach. Text B is a police officer talking to the victim of a burglary. The text annotations will help you to start thinking about the language used.

Text A ──┐

The stallholder wants the boys to play the game. He greets them in a friendly, informal, even cheeky way even though they are strangers.

SH: <u>You havin a go boys</u>, see what you can nick can I show you this one before you go. No money (.) show you this one mate no money we don't charge owt to listen before you go speak to me

Boy A: <u>I might as well</u>, how much is it

SH: <u>It's a dead easy game mate</u> it's 50p mate you get 3 shots all you've got to do mate is knock over the golf tee to win (.) get a prize if you lose mate (3.0) that's it are you havin a go

Boy A: <u>Yeah</u>

SH: <u>Mates not havin a go as well</u>

Boy B: No

Boy C: Got no cash

Boy B: Got no dosh

Boy A starts off more formally. He uses the full form 'I might as well', rather than ellipsis 'Might as well'.

Text B

Officer: <u>Hello there how are you?</u>

Victim: Oh hiya I'm fine thank you are you?

Officer: Yes fine thanks now then <u>my name's PC Dawes</u> and I understand you've got an incident to report

Victim: <u>Oh erm yeah that's right</u> I'm the lady who was burgled

Officer: <u>Ah yes I remember (0.5) well if you'd like to come into this room we could perhaps discuss the event somewhere a little quieter</u>

Victim: Oh yeah that's fine

Officer: Right then are you able to tell me what happened?

Victim: Erm (0.5) well, I was lying in bed and erm I sensed I thought I heard Ben barking he's my dog He was barking quite loudly

Officer: And when was this?

Victim: It was (0.5) it happened yesterday last night in fact I was lying in bed erm I think (0.5) I think it was probably about 11:00pm

Officer: Okay

Victim: // It's hard to //

Officer: // And what did // you think when your dog was barking?

> The police officer uses a friendly but formal greeting as he is there to conduct an interview.

1 Write a sentence about each of the underlined sections in both conversations, commenting on the level of formality and how it is appropriate for the context.

2 What is the relationship between the speakers in each conversation (the tenor)? Who is 'in charge' of each conversation?

3 Write a paragraph about the relationship between the speakers in each conversation and how this affects the language used. What is the aim of each of the speakers? How do they feel?

The conversations above have different **purposes**. The stallholder is trying to persuade the boys to play the game; the police officer is getting information from the victim. Social conversations – conversations between friends, or colleagues chatting – tend to be informal. Conversations that have a practical purpose are often more formal, though not in every case, as Text A demonstrates.

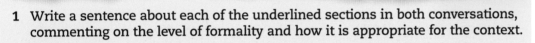

Activity 2

Read the transcript below. This short exchange took place in a shop.

1 Do the speakers use the same register throughout the exchange?

2 Can you find an example of formal language?

3 Why is the speaker formal at this point?

4 Can you find examples of informal language?

5 Why are the speakers informal at these points?

> Young man: Just these, mate
> Shopkeeper: Are you eighteen
> Young man: Um yeah hang on (*gets out his driving licence*)
> Shopkeeper: (*Looks at driving licence*) Cheers mate there you go
> Young man: Cheers

Activity 3

Read the conversation below, looking particularly carefully at A's contribution.

A: Erm (.) I seem to be (.) a bit lost. I'm trying to get to York.

B: Oh (.) oh well that's quite straightforward from here (.) if you just carry on down this road this is Heslington Lane // (.) // just

A: // Yeah //

B: carry on straight ahead // (.) the // road

A: // Yeah //

B: forks to the left but (.) ignore that just go straight ahead (.) and that's Broadway (0.5) when you come to the end of Broadway there are a set of traffic lights

A: Yes how far's that

B: Oh (0.5) mile (.) probably

1 **What is the topic and purpose of the conversation? Give two examples of how these two factors influence the language used.**

2 **What is the relationship between the speakers? Give an example of how this influences the type of language used.**

3 **What is the register of the conversation? Again, support your conclusion with examples of formal or informal language.**

Sometimes the purpose of spoken language is to keep in touch with people and build relationships with them. When we do this, we use a lot of informal expressions to express or reinforce our relationship with the other person, such as 'Hi. How are you?' We might also use language that allows us to connect with the other person, like slang or dialect.

Activity 4

Look at the exchange between two friends who have met in town.

A: Hiya you OK
B: Good morning
A: What you doing
B: I'm going shopping
A: What for
B: I'm not certain what I want to buy yet

1 **Does anything seem odd about their conversation? Why? Write down your reasons.**

2 **Imagine A and B are teenagers. Rewrite the transcript so that the language used is realistic. Write a sentence to explain each of your changes – what factors have influenced your choices?**

Here is an example of a controlled assessment task you could be expected to answer.

You will be expected to comment on how the purpose of the spoken language affects the way it is used.

Using two examples of spoken language, comment on the way teenagers adapt their spoken language to suit the situation.

You should comment on:
• how the purpose of the spoken language affects the way it is used
• how language use influences other speakers and listeners
• the level of formality
• the use of slang
• who speaks most if there is more than one speaker.

(24 marks)

Activity 5

Write a response to the following question:

Using two different examples of teenagers' spoken language (one when they are talking with their friends outside school and one when they are talking with their teachers in class), comment on some of the ways the purpose of the spoken language affects the way they speak.

You should spend 20 minutes on this question.

ResultsPlus
Self assessment

Before you complete this self-assessment activity, you might like to read some sample answers to this task on the following pages (166-167).

1 **Check your answer to Activity 5:**
   • Did you give examples of spoken language features?
   • Did you explain how these features relate to the purpose of the spoken language?
   • Have you developed this explanation clearly?

2 **Now decide which Band your answer to Activity 5 should fall into by applying the mark scheme that follows. You will need to be careful and precise in your marking.**

Band 3
• clearly explains how spoken language works
• explains how and why spoken language may change depending on the situation
• includes some examples
• shows understanding of how other people may respond to another person's spoken language, and why.

Band 4
• explains in detail how spoken language works
• explains in detail how and why spoken language changes depending on the situation
• includes good examples to support what you have said
• explains in detail how and why other people may respond to other people's spoken language, and why.

Band 5
• explains in detail how and why spoken language works
• explains in detail how and why spoken language changes depending on the situation
• includes good examples to support the various different ways these changes occur, and why
• explains in detail how and why other people may respond to other people's spoken language, and why different people may respond in different ways.

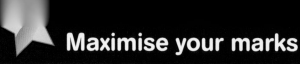

Maximise your marks

Using two examples of spoken language, comment on the way teenagers adapt their spoken language to suit the situation.

Here are three student answers to the writing about spoken language task on page 165. Read the answers, together with the examiner comments. Then complete the activity at the bottom of page 167.

Shows the ways in which spoken language works.

Teenagers will probably be more casual when they are talking with their peers, using slang, maybe swearing, but even then, their language will vary from situation to situation. My first example is a group of close friends talking. They know each other very well, the turn taking is very smooth with no interruptions and very little overlap. They use a lot of ellipsis and incomplete forms, for example when Stu says 'It was (.) you know', and Ben and Adam say 'Yeah' because they understand what he is saying. He doesn't need to say any more. When Stu is discussing his work with his teacher, there is much less of this ellipsis. She says a lot more than he does. Stu listens and uses non-verbal sounds like 'mm' or makes short responses like 'yeah'.

A good point supported by a very good example.

Examiner summary

This part of the answer is typical of a grade B performance. The student shows that they know spoken language will vary in a range of ways and they don't make the simplistic point that teenagers will speak casually when talking to their peers and formally to teachers. The student makes the very good point that close friends often don't need to say a lot to understand each other (they can use what is called 'implicit language').

Awareness that casual forms of language exist across all groups, and that there are similarities among the groups in the language they use.

The features of casual language are not very different across age groups. People will use more non-standard forms, they will use slang and they may swear. When a group of teenagers are talking together, particularly if they are friends, they will do all of these things. The slang that teenagers use will be different from the slang that older people use. My male friends, for example, call each other 'bruv' and 'blud'. The females don't use greeting or naming terms like this, but will use affectionate terms like 'babes' for their friends. In class, we don't use these forms, even when talking to our friends, unless it is a private conversation that the rest of the class and the teacher won't hear. We refer to each other by our first names (or the females do). Some of the boys refer to each other by their surnames. We call the teacher by their full name, using Mr or Miss and their surname.

Examples of language used in teenage groups that is unlikely to occur in older groups, with comment on their use, social context and meaning.

Clearly shows how use of language will change according to context as well as the person addressed.

Examiner summary

This answer has focused on a very important aspect of language in groups: how we name each other. Each example given is accompanied by a clear explanation that also shows an understanding of the way spoken language changes according to context. The comments about the way terms of address change as teenagers move from outside the school to the classroom are particularly good.

Clear statement of the point to be covered, which the student then goes on to give examples of.

Everyone adapts their language depending on the context. This will include the purpose of the language, the reason why someone is speaking, the topic they are talking about and the relationship between the speakers, friends, partners, colleagues, strangers etc. Teenagers are no different from anyone else in this, but they may be speaking in different contexts from adults or young children. For example, in school, a young child will be polite towards the teacher and call the teacher by their title and surname. Teenagers will have a more relaxed relationship with their teacher, as they are closer to being adults themselves. For example, in class recently, the lesson began formally with the teacher talking to us as a group and telling us what she wanted us to do. Once the lesson had started and she was talking to us individually, she used more ellipsis and short forms, saying things like, 'You OK?' And the students responded in a similar way saying things like 'Yeah.' This shows that the teacher is able to have a more equal relationship with us, even though she is an adult and is in a position of authority.

Use of terminology to explore how language is affected by relationship between speakers.

Examiner summary

This answer shows awareness of the way spoken language works and the way it changes according to context. The student starts with one situation and shows the subtle ways the changing relationship between teacher and pupil affects the way they talk to each other. The student also identifies this as something that is specific to teenagers, rather than young children or adults. The examples given are relevant and the student explains clearly what they show.

ResultsPlus
Build better answers

Move from a Grade B to a Grade A

Instead of just identifying and describing the features, of spoken language, Student 1 needs to explain in more detail why these features occur in this particular context.

Aim for a Grade A*

To achieve an A* Student 2 needs to sustain a good level of analysis for the full answer, and show a bit more awareness about how the role and status of a teenager affect language, and why their language may be different from that of other groups.

Putting it into practice

1   Discuss with a partner other situations in which teenagers might alter their language, how they might do this and why.

2   How does teenagers' language differ from adults' language? Discuss this with your partner.

6 Writing a script

This lesson will help you to...

→ understand the conventions of writing different kinds of script

Scripts are very different from spontaneous spoken language. A script is planned and carefully structured and written to convey a message or a narrative to an audience.

Scripts can be written for the stage, for TV or big screen, for radio and for graphic novels. They can be written for any genre, for example, soap operas, comedy, monologue and crime drama.

There are several important parts to a script:

- **Setting** – the script will contain information about where the drama is set, the time of day and, if it is for the screen, possibly even the weather. It will also give some information about the characters.

- **Directions** – the script will give instructions about who is on the stage or screen, how they move about, entrances and exits. A screenplay will give camera instructions like close ups.

- **Characters' words** – a script will contain the exact words each character says. A graphic novel will also give the text for captions which may give information about time ('Next day', 'Later'), narrative, voiceover, etc.

There are different conventions for setting out scripts, graphic novels, screenplays and stage plays. You must be clear about which you are writing as this will affect the content and the format of the script.

Activity ❶

Read the three different examples of scripts that follow (Texts A to C).

1   For each script, identify three conventions of script-writing for this form. What are the differences between a graphic novel, TV script and stage script?

Text A: Graphic novel script

Vladek narrates his story to his son Art.

[Frame: Past. In the ghetto prison]

Voiceover caption: We were maybe 200 people together waiting… Each Wednesday went vans to Auschwitz. When we were caught, it was then maybe a Thursday.

VLADEK: Look, Anja! That's my cousin, Jakov Spiegelman, in the courtyard. (Shouting out of the window) Hey! Jakov! Help! Jakov – HELP US!

JAKOV: Vladek?! There's nothing I can do!

Voiceover caption: I made signs to show I could pay. Some gold I hid in the chimney of our bunker when they took us. But a few valuables I had still with me.

JAKOV (shouting): Okay! Don't worry! Haskel will come help you!

Voiceover caption: Haskel Spiegelman was another cousin.

[Frame: Present. Art and Vladek walking along the street]

ART: Wouldn't they have helped you even if you couldn't pay? I mean, you were from the same family…

VLADEK: HAH! You don't understand.

[Frame: Close up. Vladek shown from Art's point of view]

VLADEK: At that time it *wasn't* anymore families. It was everybody to take care of *himself*.

Text B: TV script

INT. GIRLS' CLOAKROOM – COLLEGE – LATE AFTERNOON

We are looking over Sarah's shoulder into the mirror. She's doing her hair. She isn't really focusing on what she's doing. She runs the comb through her hair, but she's miles away. She reacts as the door opens. Leanne and Rachel come in talking.

LEANNE

…so I'm like what is that? **What** is **that** and…

Camera is now on all three girls. Leanne sees Sarah.

LEANNE
(to Rachel)

Tell you later.

Rachel moves across to the mirror and starts inspecting her make up. There is enough room for two people, but she crowds Sarah, just a bit. Sarah starts opening her bag, putting her things away. She's off.

RACHEL

(talking into the mirror)

Hey, you, what's your name, Sarah.
Sarah glances up to meet her gaze in the mirror briefly.

SARAH

What? I was just …

She closes her bag to show she's getting out of their way. Leanne is watching, lighting a cigarette. Through this scene, Rachel's attitude is aggressive. Leanne's is neutral.

RACHEL

Debbie's assignment. *(off Sarah's puzzled look).* The essay title. The one Debbie gave us. Did you write it down?

SARAH

Oh! Yes. It's…

(digs in her bag)

She holds a piece of paper out to Rachel. Rachel takes it, looks at it then puts it in her own bag. Leanne moves towards the mirror. Rachel and Sarah make way for her. Leanne starts doing her hair. Like Rachel, she talks to Sarah through the mirror.

LEANNE
(to Sarah)
You coming to Adam's party? Friday?

SARAH

Adam's…? I mean, he didn't…invite…

Rachel is looking at Leanne. Is Leanne serious? She's waiting for the joke.

LEANNE
(impatient)

He asked everyone in the group. *(Shrugs)* You can come with me and Raich if you want.

Rachel is furious, but daren't show it. Sarah is amazed. She's pleased Leanne has asked her, but she isn't sure. Are they making fun of her?

Rachel and Leanne leave. Sarah stays in front of the mirror. She seems undecided, then she smiles slightly. She's pleased. She goes back to combing her hair, watching herself in the mirror.

SARAH

Nick, do you want to come to Adam's…no… My friends are having a party, do you…Hey, there's a party on Friday. Do you want…

Text C: Stage script

The SCENE represents the interior of Hobson's Boot Shop in Chapel Street, Salford.

The shop windows and entrance from the street occupy the left side. Facing the audience is the counter, with exhibits of boots and slippers, behind which the wall is filled with racks containing boot boxes. Cane chairs in front of the counter. There is a desk down L with a chair. A door R leads up to the house. In the centre of the stage is a trap leading to the cellar where work is done. There are no elaborate fittings. There are gas brackets in the windows and walls...

Setting the scene

Sitting behind the counter are Hobson's two younger daughters, ALICE who is twenty-three, and VICTORIA, who is twenty-one, and very pretty. ALICE is knitting and VICTORIA is reading. They are in black, with neat black aprons. The door opens, and MAGGIE enters. She is Hobson's eldest daughter, thirty.

ALICE:	Oh, it's you. I hoped it was father going out.
MAGGIE:	It isn't. *(She crosses and takes her place at the desk).*
ALICE:	He *is* late this morning.
MAGGIE:	He got up late. *(She busies herself with an account book).*
VICKEY:	*(reading)*: Has he had breakfast yet, Maggie?
MAGGIE.	Breakfast! With a Masons' meeting last night?
VICKEY:	He'll need reviving.
ALICE:	Then I wish he'd go and do it.
VICKEY:	Are you expecting anyone, Alice?
ALICE:	Yes, I am, and you know I am, and I'll thank you both to go when he comes.
VICKEY:	Well, I'll oblige you, Alice, if father's gone out first, only you know I can't leave the counter till he goes.

Stage directions

(ALBERT PROSSER enters from the street. He is twenty-six, nicely dressed, as the son of an established solicitor would be. He crosses to the counter and raises his hat to Alice).

The dialogue within a script needs to be appropriate for the context. It needs to be suitable for the topic, purpose and mode of the speech (see page 158 for definitions of these terms). It also needs to reflect the identity of the speakers and their relationship.

Activity 2

Look back at Text A, the graphic novel script. It is an extract from *Maus* by Art Spiegelman, a story about Vladek, a Polish immigrant to the USA, who survived time in a concentration camp during the Second World War. He is telling his son Art about his attempts to escape by bribing the guards.

1 How does the writer make the dialogue seem realistic?

2 What important narrative information does the speech give?

3 What do we learn about Vladek? What do we learn about the way people in the ghetto behaved?

4 Why do the words for Vladek use standard English in the past, but not in the present? Remember that he is originally of Polish nationality.

Often the speech within a script will need to establish key features of a plot which will develop later on.

Activity 3

Look back at Text B, the extract from the TV script *Only Darkness* by Danuta Reah. Here, the character Leanne feels some sympathy for Sarah and encourages her to attend a college party. However, this has unintended and tragic consequences for Sarah later in the story which lead to further narrative developments.

1 Write a short script (no more than ten lines) in which two friends are discussing their plans for the evening. These plans are going to have disastrous consequences, but your characters are not aware of this at this stage. When writing, think about the following:

a) The form of your script: stage, screen or graphic novel? Remember to use the correct layout.

b) Where they are having this conversation: include stage directions to set the scene.

c) The identity of the friends: are they male or female? How old are they? How will this affect their spoken language?

d) How will you convey details about character and plot which will have implications at a later point in your script?

Because scripted language is planned, words can be chosen to achieve a certain effect, such as to create atmosphere or to show relationships between characters.

Activity 4

Look back at Text C, the stage script from the play *Hobson's Choice* by Harold Brighouse.

1 What are the attitudes and feelings of each of the characters? Pick out examples of stage directions and some features of the language used which tell us these things.

2 Script the next ten lines of this play. Make sure you:

a) Use the correct layout and include at least one relevant stage direction in keeping with the play

b) Use the same formal style of speech used by the family and attempt to maintain the personalities of the characters that have already been suggested.

7 Writing speeches

→ understand the basic conventions of structuring and writing a speech

A speech is written to be spoken by one person to a group of people. Audiences don't participate in speeches, though they may respond to them. Speeches can be written to give information, but usually they are written with a persuasive purpose, to convince the members of an audience that the speaker's beliefs are right.

A good speech will contain a narrative that takes the audience from where they are now to where the speaker wants them to be.

Activity 1

Read the following extract from Winston Churchill's speech to the British nation when the Nazis had defeated the Allied forces in a battle at one point during the Second World War, in 1940. Britain was facing the real possibility of Nazi invasion.

> I have, myself, full confidence that if all do their duty, if nothing is neglected, and if the best arrangements are made, as they are being made, we shall prove ourselves once again able to defend our Island home, to ride out the storm of war, and to outlive the menace of tyranny, if necessary for years, if necessary alone. At any rate, that is what we are going to try to do. That is the resolve of His Majesty's Government – every man of them. That is the will of Parliament and the nation. The British Empire and the French Republic, linked together in their cause and in their need, will defend to the death their native soil, aiding each other like good comrades to the utmost of their strength.

1 **What story is Churchill telling the British people about the development of the war? What outcome are we expecting?**

Speeches also have conventions. These often include:

- **rhetorical questions** – questions that don't require an answer, usually because the answer is obvious
- **figurative language** – simile, metaphor, personification
- **triads** (lists of three) – these can be words, phrases or whole sentences
- **repetition** – repeating an idea to emphasise it
- **facts and figures** – data, percentages and dates to support ideas
- **celebrity endorsement** – using famous people to support an idea
- use of **personal pronouns** and **direct address** – the use of 'I' to emphasise the speaker's commitment; the use of 'we' or 'our' to include the audience; the use of 'you' to affect the audience directly.

Activity 2

The speech below was given by Barack Obama when he was inaugurated as President of the United States on 20 January 2009. You can watch the video of him delivering this speech on the ActiveTeach.

> My fellow citizens:
>
> I stand here today humbled by the task before us, grateful for the trust you have bestowed, mindful of the sacrifices borne by our ancestors. I thank President Bush for his service to our nation, as well as the generosity and cooperation he has shown throughout this transition.
>
> Forty-four Americans have now taken the presidential oath. The words have been spoken during rising tides of prosperity and the still waters of peace. Yet, every so often the oath is taken amidst gathering clouds and raging storms. At these moments, America has carried on not simply because of the skill or vision of those in high office, but because We the People have remained faithful to the ideals of our forebears, and true to our founding documents. So it has been. So it must be with this generation of Americans.
>
> That we are in the midst of crisis is now well understood. Our nation is at war, against a far-reaching network of violence and hatred. Our economy is badly weakened, a consequence of greed and irresponsibility on the part of some, but also our collective failure to make hard choices and prepare the nation for a new age. Homes have been lost; jobs shed; businesses shuttered. Our health care is too costly; our schools fail too many; and each day brings further evidence that the ways we use energy strengthen our adversaries and threaten our planet.

1 Find an example of each of the following conventions in Obama's speech:

   a) a triad   b) figurative language   c) use of personal pronouns.

2 What language choices (e.g. grammar, vocabulary, sentence structure) are used in order to cater to both the audience and purpose of the speech?

3 For each convention, write a sentence stating why Obama might have chosen to use it to get his message across.

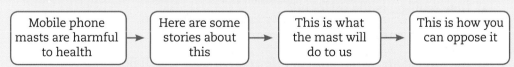

Activity 3

1 Think of a short narrative about recent events in your school or community. For example, there may be a movement to oppose the building of a mobile phone mast. The narrative would run along the lines of:

Mobile phone masts are harmful to health	→	Here are some stories about this	→	This is what the mast will do to us	→	This is how you can oppose it

2 Use your narrative to write a speech to be given to community members, or to other students in your school. Use as many of the conventions of a speech opposite as you can to persuade and influence your audience.

8 Writing dialogue

This lesson will help you to...

→ write realistic and effective dialogue within a narrative

If you choose to write a story including direct speech for your Writing for the Spoken Voice controlled assessment task you will need to be aware of the larger narrative that contains your dialogue. What happened before? What is going to happen at the end of your story? How does the narrative develop within your story? You will need to make sure these factors are reflected within your dialogue.

To create good dialogue, it needs to be appropriate for the character, it needs to be relevant to the story, and it needs a narrative purpose – it must move the story on and tell us something about the situation or the character(s). Look back at the guidance included on page 140.

Activity 1

Look at the three versions of the same narrative incident below.

A

> The house loomed above us, silhouetted against the moonlit sky.
> "I, er... I, er... I don't think... er... er... Do you - ?" stuttered Barry.
> "What on earth is the matter with you, Barry? Do you feel scared? Are you too scared to go into this house? We promised that man we met in the park that we'd come here and see if we could find out what had happened in this old, mysterious house. So that is what we're going to do. OK?"
> "I, er... I, er... I... suppose... we... er... er... er..."

B

> The house loomed above us, silhouetted against the moonlit sky.
> "I've... I've just remembered," stuttered Barry. "It's my mum's birthday. I've got to go."
> "What's the matter? Are you scared?" Terry sneered. "We said we'd go in and that's what we're gonna do."
> "OK. Come on then," said Barry, walking up to the front door and knocking loudly.

C

> The house loomed above us, silhouetted against the moonlit sky.
> "There's the house," said Barry.
> "Shall we go in?" asked Terry.
> "OK," said Barry.

1 Write a paragraph to explain which extract is the most effective in its use of dialogue. Answer the following questions to help you.ctiveness.

   a) How realistic is the dialogue?

   b) How easy is the dialogue to read and understand?

   c) How much and what kind of information does the dialogue provide aboutthe characters and their relationship?

   d) How well does the dialogue help to progress the narrative?

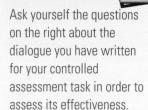

ResultsPlus
Self assessment

Ask yourself the questions on the right about the dialogue you have written for your controlled assessment task in order to assess its effectiveness.

Activity 2

Read the following extract from *Touching the Void* by Joe Simpson. Joe and Simon are trying to descend after their successful climb of the mountain Siula Grande.

There was no wind, and the snow fell silently in large heavy flakes. It was about two-thirty and we knew it would snow until late evening. We stood in silence, staring around us, trying to make out where we were.

'I think we should head down.'

'I don't know…no, not down. We must keep in touch with the ridge. Didn't you see those flutings on this side? We'd never get back up again.'

'Have we got past that second summit?'

'I think so, yes.'

'I can't see anything up there.'

The snow and cloud merged into uniform blank whiteness. I could see no difference between snow and sky further than five feet from me.

1 What does the dialogue tell you about the situation they are in?

2 Is this the way two young men in a dangerous situation would talk to each other? What does the dialogue tell us about their personalities?

3 How many reporting verbs does Joe Simpson use? Why? What is the effect?

Written dialogue can never be the same as real speech. In real life, our talk is full of imperfections that would be irritating to read on paper. However, it is possible to create the illusion of realistic dialogue by adopting a few basic techniques:

- Keep your dialogue short and snappy using short or even incomplete sentences.

- Use an appropriate register for the situation (ranging between formal and informal).

- Include colloquial phrases if they fit the character's age and background, but don't use swear words in your controlled assessment.

- Be careful with the verbs you use to report the dialogue, e.g. 'he said'. Sometimes, as in the extract above, writers don't use any at all. Most writers use a very limited range: 'said' and 'asked' are the most popular. Some writers use more descriptive words like 'called' or 'whispered' but these are often not necessary.

Results Plus
Watch out!

Dialogue in prose often uses reporting verbs such as 'cried' or 'shouted', to tell you how the words were spoken. These can be very effective, but don't overuse them, or it can seem very strange and artificial:

'Hello,' laughed Susan.

'Hello,' chortled Ann. 'How are you?' she cried.

'I'm fine,' Susan enthused.

Activity 3

Think of an event in your life when something dramatic happened. It may have been something dangerous, something new, or something particularly exciting. Try to remember what you said, and what the other people with you said. Now write about two pages telling the story of what happened, focusing on realistic dialogue to convey the atmosphere, the relationships and the emotions of the people involved and to move the story on.

8 Writing dialogue

Look at this controlled assessment task:
Write a script that contains between 30 seconds and 2 minutes of spoken language for a TV drama.

■ A Band 3 answer expresses and **develops ideas appropriately**, shows a **clear understanding** of who you are writing for and why, uses **well-chosen vocabulary**, and shows some evidence of crafting in the construction of sentences.

Detective: Where were you on the 18th July at 8.30 am?

Suspect: I was getting up, or on my way to work. I can't remember. Where were you?

Detective: (angry) You don't ask the questions. I do.

Suspect: Yeah, yeah.

Detective: We have you on CCTV talking to a man. That man was found murdered half an hour later.

Suspect: Well, I don't know anything about it.

Detective: What did you talk to him about?

Suspect: I don't remember.

Detective: (Stands up and bangs the table) What did you talk to him about!

● A Band 4 answer **effectively presents ideas in a sustained way**, and is written and structured in a way that is suitable for the chosen task, and for the appropriate audience. The words have been chosen with care and consideration, and the **writing is well controlled**, with an **appropriate variety** in the construction of sentences.

Chris and Liam stare at a blue police box that has just materialised in the street in front of them.

Chris: Can you see it too?

Liam: I… don't know. Watch out!

The door opens and a man steps out. He looks puzzled.

Dr Who: You couldn't tell me where I am?

Liam: This is Bury. (Dr Who says nothing.)

Liam: In Lancashire. (Dr Who says nothing.)

Liam: England.

Dr Who: Ah. Right. Very good. Now… Can you tell me what year it is?

Chris: Is this some kind of joke?

Dr Who: I wish it was.

▲ A Band 5 answer presents **compelling and fully developed ideas**, and is sharply focused on the audience and the purpose. The text will have an **extensive vocabulary, varied sentence forms, sustained paragraphs** and effective application of **cohesive devices**.

Outside the back of Craig's house. Night.

ROBERT: (voice-over) I don't like this.

LUKE : (Whispering fiercely) Shut up!

LUKE and ROBERT are moving along the alleyway. LUKE is in front, ROBERT following him.

ROBERT: There's a light. Look, they'll…

LUKE: Shut up! It was you who wanted to do this!

Here is an example of a controlled assessment task you could be expected to answer.

You will be expected to write in the form of a script and use the conventions of scripting.

> Write a script that contains between 30 seconds and 2 minutes of spoken language for a TV soap.
>
> (24 marks)

Activity 4

Write a response to this question:

Write the opening section of your first scene. You should focus on the conventions of a TV script.

You should spend 20 minutes on this question.

ResultsPlus
Self assessment

Before you do this self-assessment activity, you might like to read some sample answers to this task on the following pages (178-179).

1 Check your answer to Activity 4:
- Did you set out your answer using the proper conventions for a script?
- Did you include appropriate direction?
- Did you create realistic dialogue?
- Did you use the dialogue to create part of a story or narrative?

2 Now decide which Band your answer to Activity 4 will fall into by applying the mark scheme that follows. You will need to be careful and precise in your marking.

■ Band 3
- ideas are clearly expressed and suitable for the task
- the writing is mostly effective for the task and for the audience
- the dialogue is mostly realistic and effective for the story being created
- the script is properly structured with appropriate use of directions

● Band 4
- ideas are clearly and effectively expressed
- the writing is very well planned for the task and for the audience
- the dialogue is realistic, develops the narrative and creates the appropriate effects
- the script is well structured, and the directions help to set the scene and create the narrative

▲ Band 5
- ideas are fully expressed
- the writing is very well planned and appropriate for the task and audience, and the standard is sustained
- the dialogue is economical, realistic, used to drive the narrative and develop character and context
- the script is structured for the task, with directions that are appropriate for the scene and the narrative

Write a script that contains between 30 seconds and 2 minutes of spoken language for a TV soap.

Here are three student answers to the writing about spoken language task on page 177. Read the answers together with the examiner comments around and after the answers. Then complete the activity.

Student 1 – Extract typical of a grade (B) answer

Scene: (exterior, wide angles) Street at night. Passers-by. BEN waits by the bus stop for AISHA. He's looking at his watch.

Aisha: (Running towards him) Sorry, I'm sorry.

Ben: What happened?

Aisha: I couldn't get away. I think they might have guessed.

Ben: (Looks round nervously) Did anyone see you go?

Aisha: (Looks round as well) No. Said I was going to the shop.

Ben: We've got to get out of here.

Dialogue sets the scene well.

Dialogue gives important narrative information.

Examiner summary

This part of the answer is typical of a grade B performance. The script is set out using appropriate conventions and uses enough screen direction to make it clear exactly what is happening. The dialogue is realistic and shows a developing story and developing tension, without moving too fast.

Scene: The living room in the Cooper house. The TV is on. The sound is turned up LOUD. JAN is on the sofa eating chips, half watching a programme with music videos. NADINE is at the table trying to do her homework.

JAN: (Talking with her mouth full) Look at that. What's she think she's doing?

NADINE: Yeah. (She puts her hands over her ears)

JAN: (still eating chips) An that. What's she like? (Looks round at NADINE) What's up with you? Too good for us now?
(she's aggressive but she's a bit hurt by NADINE'S silence)

NADINE: (closes her book, resigned) I just want to do well.

> Directions give clear indication of the characters.

> Realistic dialogue leading up to potential confrontation.

Examiner summary

This part of the answer is typical of a grade A/A* performance. The scene of hostility between the sisters, and Nadine giving in to pressure is being subtly developed through dialogue, with support from the directions. There is, in this very short piece, clear indication of the characters and the tensions between them. The directions are appropriate, without being too detailed.

ResultsPlus
Build better answers

Move from a Grade (B) to a Grade (A)

This script needs to sustain a constant standard and develop the narrative in a way that is appropriate to the setting and the characters that appear. The scene must come to a conclusion that moves the characters on from where they are and also leads on to the next scene.

Aim for a Grade (A*)

The script must sustain a constant standard and draw the reader/viewer in. The characters must be developed in a way that is realistic and makes their responses to the situation believable. The scene must develop to a conclusion that opens up the next stage of the narrative.

Putting it into practice

1 Working in groups, perform your scripts. Is your draft script effective when it is read out?

2 Make notes of what was effective in the scripts, and what didn't work so well.

3 Amend the scripts to make them more effective.

Controlled assessment practice

Guidance for students: Spoken Language Study

What do I have to do?

You will complete one task on spoken language, from a choice of two. You must complete this task on your own.

How much time do I have?

Following preparation and research, you will have up to two hours to complete the task.

How do I prepare for the task?

You must research examples of spoken language. These may include:
- the language you hear around you
- a selection which could be taken from sources such as YouTube, TV or radio interviews, radio phone-ins, or the British Library audio archives
- your or your school's own recorded materials.

You must provide two examples of spoken language to complete the chosen task. These examples can be taken from any of the sources.

What must my response to the task show?

Your responses must show that you:
- understand how spoken language changes depending on the context, using examples
- understand some of the choices people make when they are speaking (for example: how they say it; what words or phrases they choose), using examples.

How should I present my response?

The response must allow you to show understanding of the examples of spoken language chosen. The response will be a written response of up to 1000 words to the task.

Examiner's tip

You need two examples. Try to think of two that are interesting to you and will give you material to discuss in your assessment.

Examiner's tip

You will need to comment on context and choice.

The Spoken Language Study Task for the student

You will complete one task from the two below:

EITHER
Using two examples of spoken language, comment on the way teenagers adapt their spoken language to suit the situation.

You should comment on:
- how the purpose of the spoken language affects the way it is used
- how language use influences other speakers and listeners
- the level of formality
- the use of slang
- who speaks most if there is more than one speaker. (24)

OR
Using two examples of spoken language, comment on the differences between the speech of the area where you live and the speech of different places. (You may comment on one other place or more if you choose.)

You should comment on:
- how the purpose of the spoken language affects the way it is used
- how language use influences other speakers and listeners
- the level of formality
- the use of dialect
- who speaks most if there is more than one speaker. (24)

Examiner's tip

Pick one of these tasks. Select language which will give you an opportunity to enter into a detailed analysis.

Examiner's tip

Use these bullet points to inform your response but structure your response by focusing on the most important ideas that emerge from your examples and developing the comments in detail.

Guidance for students: Writing for the Spoken Voice

What do I have to do?

You will complete one task from a choice of three.

You must complete this task on your own.

How much time do I have?

Following preparation and research, you will have up to two hours to complete this task.

How do I prepare for the task?

You should watch, read and listen to examples of the way writers create spoken words. These may include:

- radio plays
- films
- TV drama
- radio and TV documentaries
- sitcoms

- radio advertisements
- graphic novels
- monologues
- speeches
- stand-up comedy.

What must the response to the task show?

The response must show that you:
- understand how a media type (radio, TV, graphic novels, etc) works
- understand the needs of an audience and purpose.

How should I present the response?

As a written response that is effective for the form, purpose and audience chosen for the task.

Writing for the Spoken Voice Task for the student

You will complete one task from those below:

EITHER
Write a script that contains between 30 seconds and 2 minutes of spoken language for:
- a TV soap **OR**
- a graphic novel **OR**
- a radio drama.

Your script may be totally original **OR** may be for a TV soap, graphic novel or radio drama that already exists.

(24)

OR
Write a speech of up to 1000 words in support of a topic of your choice in a debate.

(24)

OR
Write a story of up to 1000 words in which direct speech is a key focus.

(24)

Examiner's tip

Select one task from these three. Use your creativity to make your writing for the spoken voice interesting.

Examiner's tip

Remember to make your spoken language appropriate for the form you're writing in.

Published by Pearson Education Limited, a company incorporated in England and Wales, having its registered office at Edinburgh Gate, Harlow, Essex, CM20 2JE. Registered company number: 872828

Edexcel is a registered trade mark of Edexcel Limited

Text © Pearson Education Limited 2010

The rights of Ron Norman, Danuta Reah, Racheal Smith and Geoff Barton to be identified as authors of this work has been asserted by them in accordance with the Copyright, Designs and Patent Act 1988.

We would like to thank Tony Farrell for his invaluable help in the development of this material.

Thanks also go to David Grant and Polly Hennessy for their contribution of additional text.

First published 2010

12 11 10
10 9 8 7 6 5 4 3 2 1

British Library Cataloguing in Publication Data
A catalogue record for this book is available from the British Library

ISBN 978 1 84690 702 9

Designed and typeset by Juice Creative Limited, Hertfordshire
Printed and bound in Great Britain at Scotprint, Haddington

Picture Credits
The publisher would like to thank the following for their kind permission to reproduce their photographs:
(Key: b-bottom; c-centre; l-left; r-right; t-top)
Alamy Images: Andrew Fox 13b, AR Photo 162, Aristidis Vafeiadakis 64, Ben Molyneux Travel Photography 108b, Bernhard Classen 38, Blickwinkel 174, British Retail Photography 80, Clive Tagg 131, Dan De Kleined 78, David J Green 33, dbImages 136 (park bench), Eric Nathan 114l, Fog Stock 118, Friedrich Stark 39, Gianni Muratore 84, Images-USA 136 (clown), Imagesource 100, Jeff Morgan 13 141, 146c, Jenny Matthews 136 (policewoman), MBI 136 (boy), Mint Photography 13t, Ourlifeimages 96, Peter Alvey 114r, Rt Images 108l, 163, S Forster 83, Stephen Frink Collection 74, Stock Connection Blue 70, VStock 169, Wave RF 107, Yadid Levy 136 (punk); **Camera Press Ltd**: Robert Doisneau 151t; Corbis: Francis G Mayer 126; **Getty Images**: AFP 105, Hulton Archive 172, Jupiter Images 15t, Kiyoshi Ota 37, Sport 116t, Ben Stansall / Stringer 151c; **iStockphoto**: 134b, 146, 164, Ekaterina Monakhova 160, Elkor 134t, Gary Sandy 138, Joe Gough 61, Marco Onofri 128r, Marek Slusarczyk 127; **Kobal Collection Ltd**: Colombia 15b; **Pearson Education Ltd**: Digital Vision 132, Imagesource 30, Photodisc 47, Photodisc / Photolink 63, Photolink / S Wanke 128l; **Reuters**: Jason Reid 173; **Rex Features**: Backpage Images 48r, Channel 4 94, Don Hammond / Design Pics Inc 11b, Garo / Phanie 136 (office worker), Imagesource 41, Mark Pain 48l, NBUC Photobank 59, Novastock 11t, Picture Perfect 34, Trent Warner 116b; **Thinkstock**: Digital Vision 86, Hemera 62, iStockphoto 136 (old lady), 154, 157, 170, Lifesize 136 (man in suit); **Veer**: Martin Crowdy 151b
Cover images: *Front:* iStockphoto: Krzysztof Kwiatkowski

All other images © Pearson Education

Every effort has been made to trace the copyright holders and we apologise in advance for any unintentional omissions. We would be pleased to insert the appropriate acknowledgement in any subsequent edition of this publication.

Acknowledgements
We are grateful to the following for permission to reproduce copyright material:

Images Poster on page 12 from "Don't be the next victim" poster, http://www.crimestoppers-uk.org/webimages/regional/Cheshire/Knife1sml.gif, copyright © Crimestoppers Trust; Page spread on page 16 from 'Best job by degrees', JobFresh (*South Yorkshire*) pp.14-15, copyright © EMP plc, publishers of Jobfresh, www.jobfresh.co.uk; Poster on page 25 'Hot water burns like fire' Children's Burns Trust, http://www.cbtrust.org.uk, Image and wording used by permission of Reliance Water Controls Ltd; Poster on page 25 from "We Crush all of this..into this" Innocent poster, http://virtualeconomics.typepad.com/photos/uncategorized/2007_we_crush_all_this_big_2.jpg, copyright © Innocent Ltd; Poster on page 51 from Global warming? leaflet by The Heartland Institute www.heartland.org, copyright © Heartland Institute.

Logos Logo on page 17 from Cancer Research UK, www.cancerresearchuk.org/, copyright © Cancer Research UK.

Screenshots Screenshot on page 14 from Club 18-30 website screenshot, http://www.club18-30.com, copyright © Club 18-30, Thomas Cook; Screenshot on page 19 from The Bobby Moore Fund, www.cancerresearchuk.org/bobbymoorefund copyright © Cancer Research UK & Bobby Moore Fund; Screenshots on pages 21, 27, 43 from EuroTrip, www.eurotrip.com; Screenshot on page 33 from "Common Problems, Self Image", http://www.youth2youth.co.uk/common_image.htm, copyright © Youth2Youth. Peer Helpline for 11-19 years old, 020 8896 3675, open every Monday and Thursday evening from 6.30pm to 9.30pm, www.youth2youth.co.uk; Screenshot on page 55 from http://www.greenpeace.org.uk/climate

Text Extract on page 11 adapted from "Is Google Making Us Stupid?" by Nicholas Carr, published in The Atlantic, July/August 2008, copyright © Nicholas Carr; Extract on page 13 adapted from "Meet the dairy farmer who pampers his 'happy' cows with waterbeds and flat-screen TVs", *The Daily Mail*, 16 May 2008, copyright © Solo Syndication; Extract on page 14 from Leo Horoscope, *Mizz Magazine*, No 631, p.55, Mizz® is a registered trademark of Panini UK Ltd; Interview on page 17 from June 2009 podcast, http://info.cancerresearchuk.org/news/podcast/transcripts/june-2009-transcript, copyright © Cancer Research UK; Extract on page 30 from *Pies and Prejudice*: In Search of the North, published by Ebury Press (Stuart Maconie), Reprinted by permission of The Random House Group Ltd; Extract on page 34 from 'children's TV programme Yo Gabba Gabba!', NME, 25 July 2009, pp.28-29, copyright © ME/IPC+ Syndication; Extract on page 37 from "High School Musical" Review by Christopher Null, 18 May 2006, http://www.filmcritic.com/reviews/2006/high-school-musical/, copyright © Christopher Null; Extract on page 38 from "Can Games Save Lives?", *Games TM magazine*, Issue 85, p.21, copyright © Imagine Publishing Ltd; Extract on page 39 from 'She's working herself out of poverty........Yeah, Right' War on Want, http://www.waronwant.org, copyright © War on Want; Extract on page 41 adapted from 'Terror', *FourFourTwo*, August 2009, p.57, copyright © Haymarket Publishing Services Ltd; Extract on page 47 '10 Oscar Nominees Per Year?' by Chris Hewitt, 25 June 2009, http://www.empireonline.com/empireblog/Post.asp?id=569, copyright © Empire/Empire Online; Extract on page 54 from 'You don't need to forsake your fun in the sun to help combat climate change', *The Times*, 17 November 2007 (Knight, J.), copyright © The Times, 2007 www.nisyndication.com; Extract on page 58 adapted from Kaiser Chiefs, Carling Live 24 @ Brixton Academy, London, 28 April 2006 by Ben Murray, http://www.musicomh.com/music/gigs/kaiser-chiefs-2_0406.htm, copyright © musicOMH; Extract on page 61 from "Why the unfair Premier League must either introduce a salary cap, or force the big five's players to drink Guinness at half-time", *The Mirror*, 22 October 2009 (Winwood, I.), copyright © Mirrorpix 2009; Extract on page 68 from "Raising the school leaving age to 18", 6 November 2007 http://www.direct.gov.uk/en/Nl1/Newsroom/DG_071319, © Crown copyright; Extract on page 79 from "Banksy Summer show official" 12 June 2009,